SPIRITUAL
GIFTS

Lessons from the Source

CHARLOTTE E. MERTZ

WESTBOW
P R E S S®
A DIVISION OF THOMAS NELSON
& ZONDERVAN

WestBow Press books may be ordered through booksellers or by contacting:

WestBow Press
A Division of Thomas Nelson & Zondervan
1663 Liberty Drive
Bloomington, IN 47403
www.westbowpress.com
844-714-3454

Because of the dynamic nature of the Internet, any web addresses or links contained in
this book may have changed since publication and may no longer be valid. The views
expressed in this work are solely those of the author and do not necessarily reflect the
views of the publisher, and the publisher hereby disclaims any responsibility for them.

Any people depicted in stock imagery provided by Getty Images are models,
and such images are being used for illustrative purposes only.
Certain stock imagery © Getty Images.

Unless otherwise indicated, all Scripture quotations are taken from the Holy Bible,
New International Version®, NIV®. Copyright © 1973, 1978, 1984 by Biblica,
Inc.™ Used by permission of Zondervan. All rights reserved worldwide.

Scripture quotations marked (AMP) are taken from the Amplified Bible, Copyright ©
1954, 1958, 1962, 1964, 1965, 1987 by The Lockman Foundation. Used by permission.

Scripture quotations marked (KJV) are taken from King
James version of the Bible, public domain.

Scriptures marked NASB are taken from the NEW AMERICAN STANDARD
BIBLE®, Copyright © 1960, 1962, 1963, 1968, 1971, 1972, 1973, 1975,
1977, 1995 by The Lockman Foundation. Used by permission.

ISBN: 979-8-3850-0449-2 (sc)
ISBN: 979-8-3850-0450-8 (e)

Library of Congress Control Number: 2023914262

Print information available on the last page.

WestBow Press rev. date: 08/08/2023

Contents

Preface

"Every good and perfect gift is from above,
coming down from the Father of the heavenly lights,
who does not change like shifting shadows."
(James 1:17)

You may notice that some of the spiritual gifts listed in the table of contents are not specifically mentioned in any of the lists found in scripture. Those listed in the Bible are offered as *examples* of the many available to the Church, which become evident as we read through the Gospels and see them applied through the lives and writings of the apostles.

Many of the spiritual gifts overlap or may be used in conjunction with other gifts, either our own or those used by other people. There may be others, as well, that I have failed to identify. I have drawn directly from scripture to show how each of the gifts discussed here

- reflects a quality of God,
- appeared in the Old Testament,
- appeared in the life and ministry of Jesus, and
- was manifested in the New Testament Church after the coming of the Holy Spirit.
- An additional section of each gift chapter includes specific scriptural teachings regarding use of the gift.

This commentary can be used either by individual readers in their personal studies or in group settings. In either case, although the commentary may be read without looking up each cited passage, I recommend reading the scripture passages in their entirety to get full benefit from the study. This will allow the Holy Spirit to provide additional insights according to each reader's understanding.

Most direct quotations have been drawn from the New International Version of the Bible, though I have also used a few (so noted) from alternative translations. Particularly in group settings, I encourage the comparative readings of multiple Bible translations to allow for further insights when wordings differ.

For the benefit of those who prefer to locate cited scriptures before reading the commentary, a list of the scriptures cited is included at the beginning of each chapter. These lists are broken down by section, corresponding to the sections of the commentary within which they are used. This should simplify breaking down each chapter to be studied in multiple sessions, if so desired. In group studies, specific passages may be assigned to be read aloud by various members of the group.

May the Holy Spirit continue to work through this study as He presents doors of opportunity and stirs up the spiritual gifts within you as you pursue them.

Chapter 1

INTRODUCTION TO SPIRITUAL GIFTS

Definition: Spiritual gifts represent attributes of the Spirit of God, translated into a form that humanity can use in service to God and His people.

Scriptures cited in Chapter 1 – Introduction

What do we know about the Holy Spirit?
Matthew 7:18, 20
Galatians 5:22-23
Romans 1:20
Galatians 5:19-21
Romans 8:5-9

How do Spiritual gifts differ from natural abilities?
Acts 2:13-41;
Acts 4:1-22;
Acts 5:1-11, 17-40;
Acts 6:1-7,
Acts 6:9-7:60;
Acts 8:1-3;
Acts 9:1-18, 23-25, 29-30;
Acts 12:1-10;
Acts 13:8-12, 45-52;
Acts 14:5-7, 19-20;
Acts 15:37-41
Acts 16:19-34,
Acts 17:5-9, 13-14;
Acts 18:12-16;
Acts 19:23-41;
Acts 20:3;
Acts 21:27-35;
Acts 23:12-24
1 Peter 4:12-19

How do we receive Spiritual gifts, what is their source, and who can receive them?
Psalm 65:4
Psalm 68:35
Joel 2:28-32
Luke 3:21-22

Luke 4:1-13
Luke 4:14-21
Isaiah 61:1-2
John 7:38-39
John 20:21-22
Acts 1:4-5
Acts 2:1-4
Acts 8:14-17
Acts 8:18-21
1 Timothy 5:22
Luke 3:22
Acts 9:17-18
Acts 10:44-47
1 Corinthians 12:18
1Thesselonians 1:4-5
Hebrews 2:3-4
James 1:17
2 Timothy 1:6

How do we discover what Spiritual gifts we have?
John 14:26
Acts 2:14
John 21:15-17
John 21:19
Acts 3:2-6
Acts 9:15-16
Acts 9:19-21
Acts 20:22-23
1 Corinthians 12:4-30

How does a believer recognize counterfeit gifts and false teachings?
Matthew 7:15-23
Proverbs 12:5
Proverbs 13:5

Proverbs 14:2
Proverbs 16:7
John 10:37
John 10:38
1 Corinthians 12:3
1 John 4:1-6
2 Corinthians 11:4
2 Corinthians 11:13-15
Colossians 2:18-23
1 Corinthians 14:37-38
Mark 3:24-25
1 Thessalonians 5:21
2 Thessalonians 2:9-12
1 Timothy 6:3-5
Titus 1:15-16
Jude 1:4, 8-10, 16-19

What should be done about counterfeit gifts and false teachings?
Acts 15:1-21
Acts 20:29-31
Ephesians 5:11
Acts 21:21-24
1 Thessalonians 5:20-22
2 Thessalonians 2:15
Thessalonians 3:6
Philippians. 1:15-18
1 Timothy 1:3-4
1 Timothy 4:1-7
1 Timothy 6:11-12
1 Timothy 6:20-21
2 Timothy 3:1-9
Titus 1:10-14
2 John 1:9-11
Jude 1:20-23

Where and how can we start putting our gifts to use?
1 Peter 4:10
Matthew 25:14-23
2 Corinthians 9:10-11

3

Chapter 1
Introduction to Spiritual Gifts

> *Definition: Spiritual gifts represent attributes of the*
> *Spirit of God, translated into a form that humanity can*
> *use in service to God and His people.*

We have all had questions about the gifts of the Holy Spirit. If you didn't, you wouldn't be reading this book. If I didn't, I never would have written it. Even as I write, the Lord continues to reveal to me answers to questions I hadn't even known to ask.

What are Spiritual gifts? The Bible lists some specific gifts as examples of how God's people are gifted. But is that all there are? How can we know what is a Spiritual, super-natural gift and what is just a natural interest or ability? Most of us have seen evidence of supernatural gifting that is used for ungodly purposes; how can we know what gifts are from God and what is not?

These are some of the questions that led me to this study of Spiritual gifts. Perhaps you have some of the same questions.

Join me as we discover the working of the Holy Spirit not only in the New Testament Church but in Jesus' own ministry and even in the days before Jesus was born. We will learn about a wide variety of the Holy Spirit's gifts, how they can most effectively be used, and how we can help enrich God's Kingdom as we, and those around us, discover and apply our Spiritual gifts.

I encourage you to take time to read in full the passages cited, in whatever translation of the Bible you have. You may also wish to compare translations to consider the variations of wording you may encounter. A different translation may clarify a question you have or provide additional insight into what the writer was trying to express. The deeper we dig into the Word, the better we come to understand what the Lord has to say to us.

Let us begin by recognizing that Spiritual gifts represent attributes of the Spirit of God Himself. Since they do, as we ask about the gifts of the Holy Spirit, we must also ask ourselves about the Giver of those gifts.

What do we know about the Holy Spirit?

We are told in Matthew 7:18, 20 that "A good tree cannot bear bad fruit, and a bad tree cannot bear good fruit.... Thus, by their fruit you will recognize them[1]." So we must ask, "What is the fruit of the Holy Spirit?"

Galatians 5:22-23 lists the fruit of the Spirit as love, joy, peace, patience, kindness, goodness, faithfulness, gentleness, and self-control. Romans 1:20 tells us that "since the creation of the world His invisible attributes, His eternal power and divine nature, have been clearly seen, being understood through what has been made, so that they are without excuse." Therefore, we can expect the Spirit not only to produce His own attributes in the people in whom He dwells but also to express those traits through the gifts He bestows on His people. We can expect the gifts to be an extension of the Spiritual fruit developing in individuals. They should also promote the entire range of ministries needed throughout the world, as a witness to God's saving grace.

For the same reason, we can be assured that if, rather than producing fruit of the Spirit, something is instead producing deeds of the flesh (identified in Galatians 5:19-21 as including sexual immorality, impurity and debauchery; idolatry and witchcraft; hatred, discord, jealousy, fits of rage, selfish ambition, dissensions, factions and envy; drunkenness, orgies, and things of a similar nature), it is in opposition to the Holy Spirit and is therefore not from Him.

The New International Version of Romans 8:5-9 explains it this way: "Those who live according to the sinful nature have their minds set on what that nature desires; but those who live in accordance with the Spirit have their minds set on what the Spirit desires. The mind of sinful man is death, but the mind controlled by the Spirit is life and peace; the sinful mind is hostile to God. It does not submit to God's law, nor can it do so. Those controlled by the sinful nature cannot please God. You, however, are controlled not by the sinful nature but by the

---

[1] All scripture passages are from the New International Version unless otherwise noted. Readers are encouraged to compare these references with other translations, which may reveal further insights through differing translations of the original text.

Spirit, if the Spirit of God lives in you. And if anyone does not have the Spirit of Christ, he does not belong to Christ."

Does the Spirit of God live in you, or are you living according to your sinful nature? If you try to excuse your sin rather than repenting of it, you are rejecting the work—the conviction—of the Holy Spirit, so the Spirit of God cannot live within you. In our natural state, everyone sins; and that sin will bring about eternal suffering.

You can choose to belong to Christ by acknowledging your sinful nature, confessing your sins to Him, and recognizing that Jesus Christ, the Son of God, accepted your suffering and death sentence in your place so that you could live through eternity with Him. If you truly believe that and turn away from your sins, He will forgive your sins and you will belong to Him.

This does not mean that you will never again sin, but it does mean that you are no longer enslaved by the power of sin. It means that you will have the ability to break away from your sin nature and begin a renewed life in Christ.

If you choose to begin—to be reborn—into a new life in Christ, I encourage you to write down (visibly as well as in your mind and heart) your intention to do so, somewhere where you will be reminded of it in times of your greatest difficulties, and share the good news of your salvation with someone else. I rejoice with you!

1. How do Spiritual gifts differ from natural abilities?

Not all our activities are motivated by Spiritual giftings or the sinful flesh. Most of us have inborn talents or we develop skills and abilities through our life experiences or hard work. We can think of these as "natural abilities."

The difference between Spiritual gifts and natural abilities lies in the empowerment the Holy Spirit gives us and in a gift's effectiveness in fulfilling God's purposes. The Holy Spirit's empowerment is far beyond that of any natural ability. But we cannot know the extent of that empowerment or our effectiveness until we put our abilities to use.

Unless the Lord Himself has revealed them to us in some way (as He sometimes does through the gifts of knowledge or prophecy), we cannot know what Spiritual gifts we have until we attempt to use them. Nor can we identify them definitively as *Spiritual* gifts until we become aware of either our extraordinary empowerment or the results of our actions in light of what we were called to accomplish.

Thus, from the very beginning, the gifts must be employed by faith. We must have faith that ...

1. what the Holy Spirit is speaking to our spirits to do is *His direction* to us;

2. His direction is also His assurance that *He has empowered* us to do whatever He's calling us to do;

3. *He will honor* whatever it is He's calling us to do;

4. if we are obedient to God's direction, *it will accomplish His purpose*, even if we don't see immediate results.

But how can we be sure that it's the Holy Spirit who is speaking to our spirits, and not our human will or satanic deception?

We must test the spirits: Does it represent Biblical truth, love, or purity? Does it encourage, build, or heal? Does it glorify God?

Or does it discourage, destroy, create bondage, or bring condemnation, confusion or dissension to the Body of Christ?

If you read Acts 2:13-41; 4:1-22; 5:1-11, 17-40; 6:1-7, 9-7:60; 8:1-3; 9:1-18, 23-25, 29-30; 12:1-10; 13:8-12, 45-52; 14:5-7, 19-20; 15:37-41— regarding dissension within the ranks of the Church—; 16:19-34, 17:5-9, 13-14; 18:12-16; 19:23-41; 20:3; 21:27-35; and 23:12-24, you will discover that the greater the threat the Church's work presents to the enemy, the more determinedly Satan tries to get us off track, to discredit our ministries, and to discourage us from continuing. So be alert!

But God is faithful: In each situation in the Acts of the Apostles, God either provided a remedy or an escape, or else He used the situation in a powerful way to witness and to build the Church. So pray and watch and expect His guidance and encouragement.

The Apostle Peter wrote, in 1 Peter 4:12-19, that we should expect to share in the sufferings of Christ as we continue His work in the world. We should not expect to be shielded from all sufferings merely because we are serving God, but neither should we become discouraged from continuing to do His work and to pursue His will. As we will see in the chapter on martyrdom, suffering even in this present life can be a form of martyrdom when, through our sufferings, God's Spiritual work is accomplished.

So when you suffer, commit yourself even more fully to Christ and continue to do good.

2. How do we receive Spiritual gifts, what is their source, and who can receive them?

As we consider what the Bible itself tells us, we see that it is God who chooses His people and fills them with His good things (Psalm 65:4). It is God who gives power and strength to His people (Psalm 68:35). And the Spirit has been promised to all God's servants, unlimited by age, gender, or social or financial status (Joel 2:28-32).

The first person we see fully in-filled with the Holy Spirit in the Bible is Jesus. Jesus submitted to His Father's authority by placing Himself in the hands of John to be baptized (symbolically dying to self and being raised to the Father's complete will). He was acknowledging before others His faith and commitment to God the Father. Although He was baptized in water along with other believers, only Jesus was simultaneously filled with the Holy Spirit, who appeared in visible form and was accompanied by an audible acknowledgment of Jesus by God Himself (Luke 3:21-22). It was by being filled with the Holy Spirit that Jesus received the empowerment he needed to begin His public ministry.

The Spirit filled Jesus and continued to lead and sustain Him through the wilderness over the following days. During those forty days, as Satan tried to tempt Him into succumbing to His human nature, Jesus drew His strength and sustenance solely from the Holy Spirit. Although He "was hungry" afterwards, so presumably was physically weak, He was able to withstand His spiritual adversary by relying on the power of the Holy Spirit (Luke 4:1-13).

In Luke 4:14-21 we see Jesus beginning his public ministry, still empowered by the Holy Spirit, and hence able to announce the fulfillment of Isaiah's prophecy (Isaiah 61:1-2).

John 7:38-39 likens this long-lasting empowerment by the Holy Spirit to streams of living water, like a continuous flow from an unlimited source. Yet this empowerment was still not available to His followers in such unending streams because Jesus had not yet been glorified (v. 39).

Following His resurrection, Jesus appeared to His disciples. By breathing on His disciples in John 20:21-22, Jesus was bestowing the Holy Spirit (or breath of God), not in baptism yet but much as believers of the Old Testament had received the Holy Spirit, for a limited duration and for a specific purpose.

Acts 1:4-5, on the other hand, speaks of baptism in the Holy Spirit, a permanent empowerment by the Holy Spirit. In both these instances, Jesus was telling His disciples to be open and receptive to the Holy Spirit's work within them, assuring them that the Spirit would be available to help them accomplish what He was sending them to do.

After Jesus ascended into heaven, He fulfilled His promise, as recorded in Acts 2:1-4. It should be noted that the believers spoke in other tongues only as the Spirit enabled them, as an indication of His having come to abide within them. The extent of their speaking in other tongues was not a measure of how fully they had been filled but was merely an indication that they *had indeed been* filled.

But what of believers who were not in the Upper Room on the day of Pentecost? Acts 8:14-17 tells us that some believers in Samaria later received the Holy Spirit through prayer and laying on of hands. There is no mention in this case of an extraordinary occurrence, as there had been in the Upper Room, when what appeared to be tongues of flame and the sound of a rushing wind were apparent to all. In this case the believers simply received—actively took possession of—the Holy Spirit when it was offered to them by the laying on of hands.

One of the Samaritans had the wrong attitude. Acts 8:18-21

suggests that Simon understood neither the Source of the power nor the purpose of the laying on of hands. He may have seen the ability as a source of income or as a means of drawing people to himself. Verse 21 tells us Peter recognized that Simon's heart was not right before God. Peter therefore denied his request because Simon's purpose and motivation for using and bestowing the Holy Spirit's power were wrong.

The Apostle Paul later wrote a warning in his first letter to Timothy (1 Timothy 5:22) that the laying on of hands must be directed by the Holy Spirit. Even our good intentions are not enough because we can't see into another's heart as the Holy Spirit can. We must not act on our own initiative but must wait for the Holy Spirit's leading.

How do we receive the Spirit? Baptism in the Holy Spirit does not necessarily have to follow baptism in water. Although the disciples had been baptized before the day of Pentecost, we read in Luke 3:22 that Jesus received the Holy Spirit and water baptism on the same occasion, probably within moments of each other.

Acts 9:17-18 indicates that Saul's baptism in the Holy Spirit, before even being baptized in water, was accompanied by the healing of his blindness.

Acts 10:44-47 reports that the Holy Spirit was being poured out even on Gentiles, before water baptism could take place. This Spirit baptism was not precipitated even by the laying on of hands but occurred while Peter was still speaking. The Holy Spirit took the initiative to touch all who heard. We can only surmise that God's purpose may have been to illustrate for the believing Jews that salvation and the Holy Spirit were for all believers, not for Jews alone.

As we can see here, we can't force the Holy Spirit's working into some human-determined pattern. Likewise, we are reminded in 1 Corinthians 12:18 that it is God, not people, who decides who will receive which Spiritual gifts, and for what purposes.

But, we may ask, what is the purpose of this Spiritual baptism? 1Thessalonians 1:4-5 and Hebrews 2:3-4 assure us that the Spirit's power confirms our salvation and attests that the gospel is active in our lives.

But what is the purpose of the gifts? As we proceed through this study, we will see that all the gifts are intended to serve God or His people. Spiritual gifts might be likened to God's birthday presents given to us after we are born again. However, unlike toys that are soon outgrown and forgotten, these are meant to last a lifetime and are to be used not only to strengthen our own faith as we learn to lean more heavily on the Holy Spirit, but to bless the people around us and, ultimately, to being glory to God. For, as James 1:17 reminds us, "Every good and perfect gift is from above, coming down from the Father...."

Baptism in the Spirit and the endowment of Spiritual gifts, however, are not enough to accomplish the work God intends. In 2 Timothy 1:6, Paul entreats Timothy to "fan into flame the gift of God." Although Timothy had received, by the laying on of hands, the (unspecified) spiritual gift the Apostle Paul referred to in this passage, Timothy himself needed to take responsibility for using the gift. He had to actively take hold of the Spirit's power and apply the gift he had been given. In the same way, all of us are responsible to actively use the gifts with which the Holy Spirit has endowed us.

3. How do we discover what Spiritual gifts we have?

According to John 14:26, the Holy Spirit not only gives us the gifts but reveals them to us and guides us in their use. Sometimes He reveals the gifts only as people obey His direction and act in faith, as Peter did in Acts 2:14. At other times, empowerment is revealed through implication of a specific direction or by prophecy:

In John 21:15-17, three phrases indicate that Jesus was revealing a special empowerment to Simon Peter through his specific direction. The *directives*, "Feed my lambs," "Take care of my sheep," and "Feed my sheep," indicated that Peter was to shepherd (or pastor) both new and mature believers, teaching them and protecting them from being led astray.

As we continue reading verses 18 and 19, we see Jesus revealing that Simon Peter has been given an additional gift, which had not been evident before the Day of Pentecost. Although Peter had dodged persecution by denying the Lord three times following Jesus' arrest, Jesus' *prophecy* indicates that Peter would be given another opportunity to serve as a martyr, this time Spiritually empowered to provide an extraordinary testimony of faithfulness. The single, simple direction from Jesus, "Follow Me" (John 21:19) may have provided all the *encouragement* Simon Peter needed to remain faithful despite his human nature and natural inclinations.

When Peter told the crippled beggar, "Look at us!" in Acts 3:2-6, Peter was not asking for the man's undivided attention but was asking him to recognize that he and John had no money either. They wanted him to see that they did not put their reliance on silver and gold but in Christ. Peter and John give him what they did have: They acted on the *faith* they had in Christ's richer, longer lasting provision of healing. In this way their gift of healing was confirmed for themselves through effective use, and they provided an object lesson in faith to the crippled man, as well as providing an object lesson in the use of Spiritual gifts for us.

In Acts 9:15-16, the Lord directed Ananias through *revelation* and *prophecy*.

Saul's (the Apostle Paul's) Spiritual empowerment was revealed upon *use* when he began to preach (Acts 9:19-21).

Later, the Holy Spirit *compelled* Paul to proceed on his mission journey (Acts 20:22-23) even in the face of dire warnings of what awaited him.

A partial list of gifts is provided in 1 Corinthians 12:4-30, as examples of how the Holy Spirit empowers God's people to fulfill the service and various works He calls us to accomplish.

It would be a mistake to try to pinpoint gifts too closely, however, and to try to fit them into regimented pigeonholes separate from every other gift. Spiritual gifts tend to overlap and blend into one another so that it becomes impossible to tell where one ends and another begins. Almost all of the scriptural references to gifts are indicative of a blending of two or more. Prophecy, for instance, often incorporates edification or exhortation, tongues, or knowledge; the same person who has a gift of tongues may interpret—a form of knowledge because it is available only through Spiritual revelation; pastoring often involves teaching, edification, and exhortation; teaching often requires measures of both edification and wisdom as well as encouragement and exhortation; healing and resurrection are manifestations of a form of mercy....

Therefore, it would appear unreasonable to settle for having discovered a single Spiritual gift and stop investigating what others we might have besides. On the other hand, although each of us may have been endowed with several gifts, no one should expect to have them all.

While it may be true that we are more strongly gifted in one or more areas than in others, we should not neglect *any* of our gifts, for the Spirit has empowered us for a purpose, and if we fail to use all of our gifts, then we cannot completely fulfill God's purposes for our lives.

4. How does a believer recognize counterfeit gifts and false teachings?

Most of us don't like to have to think about dealing with counterfeiters and deceivers. But Satan is a liar and the father of lies (John 8:44) and will do what he can to deceive Christ's followers. Matthew 7:15-23 warns us to weigh carefully the actions and attitudes of those claiming to be acting on God's behalf, differentiating between the resulting fruit, whether good or bad, and recognizing the true source of each:

The Proverbs are rich in providing guidelines to help us recognize the good fruit from the bad: "The plans of the righteous are just, but the advice of the wicked is deceitful" (Proverbs 12:5). "The righteous hate what is false, but the wicked bring shame and disgrace" (Proverbs 13:5). "He whose walk is upright fears the LORD, but he whose ways are devious despises him" (Proverbs 14:2). "When a man's ways are pleasing to the LORD, he makes even his enemies live at peace with him" (Proverbs 16:7).

Jesus Himself told us in John 10:37 to use these criteria to judge whether to believe even Him, warning us not to believe Him unless His own actions, character, and purposes emulated those of God the Father. Even if we do not believe Jesus Himself, we are told that we can believe the miracles He performed to understand that He and the Father were acting in one accord, toward the same end purpose (John 10:38). 1 Corinthians 12:3 also tells us that no one who is speaking by the Spirit of God can curse Jesus; neither can anyone truly acknowledge that Jesus is the Lord unless that truth has been revealed to their hearts by the Holy Spirit.

The Apostle John wrote much the same in 1 John 4:1-6, going a step farther to identify those who deny Jesus as harboring the spirit of the antichrist. Although the world pays attention to such people, believers must not. Believers in Christ recognize the truth in Godly teaching because the Holy Spirit reveals to us the true character of God. We must take care to differentiate the Spirit of truth from the spirit of falsehood.

We should be careful about the teaching we pay attention to. In 2 Corinthians 11:4, Paul rebuked the Corinthians for accepting too readily false teachings about Jesus and the gospel. We must weigh such teachings carefully against what we know of the character and activity of the Godhead.

Paul went on to warn, in 2 Corinthians 11:13-15, that a person who misleads others in this way is like Satan himself, masquerading as something he is not, attempting to misguide believers to thwart God's greater purposes.

Similarly, some people use a pretense of humility and try to pass themselves off as believers in Christ, but their worship and faith are misplaced, and their actions are not directed by the Holy Spirit but by ideas derived from the natural mind (Colossians 2:18-23). They may make up their own rules and restrictions, but those rules are of little value because they do not change a person's sinful nature.

1 Corinthians 14:37-38 suggests that those who are truly Spiritually gifted can recognize the truth and purpose behind the exercise of others' Spiritual gifts, as well. If dissention arises between people claiming to be exercising Spiritual gifts, it should serve as a warning that at least one of the people involved is not truly working in accord with the Spirit of God. Jesus pointed out in Mark 3:24-25 that a kingdom divided

against itself will fall; therefore, it is unreasonable to believe that the Holy Spirit would work at cross purposes with Himself.

When it comes to things of the Holy Spirit, 1 Thessalonians 5:21 tells us in no uncertain terms, "Test everything. Hold on to the good."

Particularly as the end times approach, 2 Thessalonians 2:9-12 alerts us, we will see an increase in the kinds of counterfeit miracles, signs, and wonders Satan will use to deceive people who have not put their faith in Christ. God will permit their rebellious denial of the truth to pave the way for their delusion and subsequent destruction.

The teaching of false doctrine, in opposition to the gospel Jesus taught, is an indication of self-indulgence rather than commitment to God's purposes. 1 Timothy 6:3-5 points out that controversies and quarrels that arise from these teachings and that result in strife and unhealthy relationships are indicative of such deceptions and should serve as an alert to believers to ignore the people espousing those teachings.

Paul wrote to Titus (Titus 1:15-16) that those who are pure—whose outlook is from a Godly perspective—see all things as pure. But those who have succumbed to the corruption of their sinful nature perceive ugliness and corruption all around them. Although they claim to know God, they are disobedient toward Him. Such people cannot be effective in God-directed ministry. It was people like this who are described in Jude 1:4, 8-10, 16-19—speaking abusively against whatever they do not understand, being grumblers and faultfinders, following their own evil desires, boasting and flattering for their own advantage. They are divisive and follow their natural instincts rather than being directed by the Spirit.

5. What should be done about counterfeit gifts and false teachings?

When the apostles were faced with questions of accurate or false teachings in Acts 15:1-21, they sought Godly counsel and compared the question with not only what God had shown or taught them in the past through personal experience but also with scriptural prophecy and teachings.

Paul wrote in Acts 20:29-31, as he had warned the Church many times before, to be alert and watchful for distortions of truthful teachings, even by some of their own number. When error or corruption or "fruitless deeds of darkness" are discovered, Ephesians 5:11 tells us, we should expose it and have nothing to do with either encouraging or perpetuating it. When our own teaching is called into question, Acts 21:21-24 indicates that we should take steps to clarify the truth of our position while avoiding giving unnecessary offense.

We should give prophecies due consideration and test them for validity, 1 Thessalonians 5:20-22 tells us, avoiding any wrong ("evil") but retaining whatever is good. When we know the truth, we can and should stand by accurate, truthful teaching, and not be swayed by any inaccuracies we might hear (2 Thessalonians 2:15). We are warned in 2 Thessalonians 3:6 to avoid believers who do not live according to scriptural teaching.

But the Apostle Paul wrote in his letter to the Philippians (Philippians 1:15-18) that the motivation, whether selfish or unselfish, that drives someone to preach Christ is less important than the fact that the truth is taught at all.

The Apostle Paul wrote to Timothy (1 Timothy 1:3-4) that in some situations we need to give correction and reproof to those who teach false doctrines and who waste their time rather than doing God's work. He continued by encouraging Timothy that correction can be accomplished through faithful teaching and by setting a Godly example for others to follow (1 Timothy 4:1-7). Like Timothy, we are encouraged to "pursue righteousness, godliness, faith, love, endurance and gentleness," holding firmly to our faith and the promise of eternal life (1 Timothy 6:11-12), avoiding godless chatter and opposing ideas that can distort and distract us from the truth (1 Timothy 6:20-21).

In 2 Timothy 3:1-9, Paul became even more outspoken, alerting Timothy to signs of the last days, and describing a society much like what we live in today. He gave Timothy a warning that we, too, would be wise to heed—to have nothing to do with people who aggressively oppose the truth.

Titus 1:10-14 teaches that rebellious talkers and deceivers—those who appear to be believers but who reject the truth—should be rebuked sharply and silenced. We should pay no attention to the commands of those who reject the truth.

We are warned in 2 John 1:9-11 not to take into our house or welcome anyone who teaches falsehoods, since in offering false teachers the protection of our home, we are making it easier for them to promote their work.

Yet these tactics aren't the only ones we can employ to combat false teachings. Jude 1:20-23 points out that we have a responsibility to strengthen ourselves through prayer and development of our faith, remaining close to God in this life as we anticipate and prepare for the life to come. We are to be merciful and encouraging to others, extending the grace and truth of the gospel to those who are still in sin, even while we shun the sin itself.

6. Where and how can we start putting our gifts to use?

First, 1 Peter 4:10 tells us to make ourselves available to the Lord: He sets us in front of doors of opportunity that He has matched to our gifts. It's up to us to open them. We can talk to neighbors, friends, and acquaintances about Jesus; when we see a need, we should be willing to help supply it.

We shouldn't try to have the same "style" as someone else or do the same task as someone else if we don't feel God's prompting to do so. We are created in God's image. He is the creator. He expects us to be creative, innovative, and different from one another. If "Joe's" teaching filled every need and suited every student, there would be no need for "Mary" to teach. But Mary may have a different approach, which will make her successful in reaching different people in different circumstances. Both are anointed; and each has a different and important role.

It's all right to start small as we discover our Spiritual gifts and develop confidence in using them. Then, like the servants who wisely invested their master's talents to increase his resources (Matthew 25:14-23), when we are faithful in using whatever gifts we have, our ministries can grow. This principle also appears in 2 Corinthians 9:10-11, suggesting that not only may God increase the harvest by our use of the gifts, but the "store of seed" as well may be increased, implying that we might discover additional gifts that we had no idea we'd been endowed with.

As we begin to respond to the opportunities before us, we begin also to become sensitive to the Lord's leading and we become more acutely attuned to His voice. Some people hear God's voice audibly; others hear His voice within their heads—different from their own inner voice but not traversing the auditory nerve; some have visions of what He is revealing to them; and yet others simply sense a "nudge," "compulsion," or "check" in their spirit. However He speaks to you, you will probably find that by responding appropriately you will learn to recognize His directions more clearly.

Our study of the individual gifts will include both Old Testament and New Testament readings. Although there is some overlap, in general, our Old Testament study will provide illustrations of how a gift was bestowed and used (and occasionally misused or counterfeited) before Jesus sent the Holy Spirit to dwell within us, and it will give us understanding of what led to the gift's definition. The New Testament readings will provide more specific teachings about Spiritual gifts in general and individual gifts in particular, as well as providing illustrations of the gifts' use in the newly established Church.

We can observe a number of people in the Old Testament who were individually anointed by God to fulfill a unique role. Many of them showed evidence of special sensitivity and responsiveness to God's direction, some for a limited period of time, others over as much as a lifetime. The general ability of believers to draw directly from the Holy Spirit's immediate presence is not evident, however, until after Jesus' ascension into heaven. Accessing the Holy Spirit's power in the Old Testament might be compared to running on battery power, relying on continual recharging, whereas the New Testament infilling with the Holy Spirit is more like becoming hard-wired into the primary power source.

But baptism in the Holy Spirit offers much more than a constant power source. When the Holy Spirit dwells within us, we become aligned with God's Spirit and purposes, with the mind of Christ, and begin to see people and events through God's eyes. It is this extraordinary perspective that helps to guide us in knowing how and when to employ our Spiritual gifts.

Chapter 2

PREPARING OURSELVES

Purpose: The ultimate purpose of Spiritual gifts is to bring glory to God and to draw people into closer relationship with Him.

Scriptures cited in Chapter 2 – Preparing Ourselves

Introduction
1 Corinthians 10:31-33
Philippians 2:13
1 Peter 4:6-11

To what extent and in what way does the responsibility in the effective use of our Spiritual gifts lie with God?
Daniel 2:17-23
Zechariah. 4:6
John 14:10

To what extent and in what way does the responsibility in the effective use of our Spiritual gifts lie with the person using the gift?
John 14:10
James 4:2-3
1 Corinthians 4:1-5
1 Corinthians 3:10-15

To what extent and in what way does the responsibility in the effective use of our Spiritual gifts lie with the beneficiary of the gift?
James 5:14-16
Matthew 21:22
Matthew 13:58
Ephesians 4:18

What assurances does the Bible offer us in regard to Spiritual gifts?
Matthew 21:21-22
James 1:6
John 5:14-15

How can we prepare ourselves for effective use of our Spiritual gifts?
Psalm 51: 9-18
2 Peter 1:3-8

Consider the roles
Mark 9:28-29
Matthew 17:19-21
Psalm 35:13; Ps 69:10
Philippians 4:6-7
1 Chronicles 29:14-16
Psalm 138:6
Psalm 37:4
Psalm 30:9-12
Deuteronomy 8:10-18
Psalm 50:14-15
Psalm 116:12-14
Jeremiah 29:12-13
Matthew 7:8

What warnings are we given?
Judges 2:1-3
1 Chronicles 28:9
2 Chronicles 12:14
Psalm 66:18
Acts 8:18-24
Romans 8:1-2

What reminders are we offered?
Ephesians 4:1-7

Chapter 2
Preparing Ourselves

> *Purpose: The ultimate purpose of Spiritual gifts is to bring glory to God and to draw people into closer relationship with Him.*

We have determined that Spiritual gifts are given by the Holy Spirit to His people. But it is reasonable to ask *why* we have been given these special abilities. What is their ultimate purpose, and what, therefore, should our focus be when we exercise the gifts?

In 1 Corinthians 10:31-33 we are directed that in whatever we do, we are to do it for the glory of God. We are not to try to seek our own good but to help—not hinder or misguide—others as they strive to grow closer to God.

We also see that, according to Philippians 2:13, it is God who is working within all of us, leading us to desire what He desires and to act in such as way as to achieve His ultimate purposes for good.

Therefore, as 1 Peter 4:6-11 points out, the ultimate purpose of Spiritual gifts is to bring glory to God and to draw people into closer relationship with Him.

To what extent and in what way does the responsibility in the effective use of our Spiritual gifts lie with...God?

Daniel acknowledged that the primary ability comes from God (Daniel 2:17-23). "The wisdom and power are His." It is God who selects whom to empower, who directs them, and who provides them with the ability to apply the wisdom and power He puts at their disposal.

The Lord made clear to Zerubbabel (Zechariah. 4:6) that His work is not accomplished by the strength or worldly power of people but only through the power of the Holy Spirit.

Jesus, too, acknowledged in John 14:10 that even the words He spoke and the things He did were directed by God the Father. When

He promises to do whatever is asked in His name, it is on the basis that the one asking has faith in Him, just as He had faith in the Father. Having faith in Him means having faith in His purposes and His goals rather than in our own human agendas; in other words, when our hearts and minds are in alignment with His—and hence with the Father's—we work as one with them and they can readily work through us. It is easy, then, to understand and believe that He will indeed do whatever we ask in His name.

To what extent and in what way does the responsibility in the effective use of our Spiritual gifts lie with...*the person using the gift?*

So how much is really dependent upon us? As we saw in John 14:10, in order to effectively apply the gifts with which the Spirit has empowered us, we must align our purposes with God's will.

James, too, warned in James 4:2-3, that we sometimes do not receive what we ask for because our motives are selfish, not in accord with God's heart.

The Apostle Paul wrote in his first letter to the Corinthians (1 Corinthians 4:1-5) that God requires faithfulness from those to whom He has given a trust. At the appointed time, God will expose the motives of our hearts, giving praise according to our faithfulness in whatever He has entrusted us with.

1 Corinthians 3:10-15 reminds us, however, that we are responsible for applying our gifts in a worthwhile manner. Whether we use them well or carelessly will not determine whether or not we are saved, but it will determine how effective our lives are and how much difference our lives and work will make in light of eternity.

To what extent and in what way does the responsibility in the effective use of our Spiritual gifts lie with...*the beneficiary of the gift?*

A prayer offered in faith will be heard, James 5:14-16 assures us; if we do not receive it is often because we have not asked. Therefore, if we need the Spirit's power used in our behalf, we should ask for it. Matthew 21:22, too, assures us that if we believe, we will receive what we ask for in prayer.

Yet if people are unwilling to believe, Spiritual gifts cannot be used effectively. Matthew 13:58 reveals that Jesus did not perform many miracles in localities where there was an extensive lack of faith. God will not overrule faithlessness or hardened hearts. Ephesians 4:18 refers to people who had self-determined their own lack of faith. God had allowed them to remain in ignorance and darkness because they had consciously hardened their hearts against Him. Among such people, Spiritual gifts cannot be effectively used.

What assurances does the Bible offer us in regard to Spiritual gifts?

Matthew 21:21-22 teaches us that faith for miracles includes expectation of God's positive response, not just hoping but believing that God will do it (James 1:6).

The promise that we will receive whatever we ask for has often been misconstrued. If we read I John 5:14-15 carefully, we see that there is a condition set. "This is the confidence we have in approaching God: that if we ask anything *according to His will*, He hears us. And if we know that He hears us—whatever we ask—we know that we have what we asked of Him."

If our will is truly aligned with the will of God, we can be sure that God will respond positively to our request. When it applies to our effective use of the Spiritual gifts He has given to us for this very purpose, we can be assured that He will work with and through us in their effective application.

How can we prepare ourselves for effective use of our Spiritual gifts?

In order to effectively administer our Spiritual gifts, we must acknowledge that we are sinners, repent of those sins, and ask God's forgiveness. Only then can we act from pure, God-directed motives. We then exemplify what God's grace can do as he works within us. Psalm 51: 9-18 offers us a picture of true contrition, with the goals of personal cleansing, establishing motives that align with God's will and righteousness, setting a good example for others, and drawing others to God.

We are told in 2 Peter 1:3-8 that in order to "become partakers of the divine nature" we should "make every effort to add to your faith goodness; and to goodness, knowledge; and to knowledge, self-control; and to self-control, perseverance; and to perseverance, godliness; and to godliness, brotherly kindness; and to brotherly kindness, love. For if you possess these qualities in increasing measure, they will keep you from being ineffective and unproductive in your knowledge of our Lord Jesus Christ." It is a process, which takes time and commitment to develop, but every step draws us closer to our goal of knowing, understanding, and emulating Christ.

Consider the roles the following play:

Prayer and fasting:

Mark 9:28-29

28 When He came into the house, His disciples began questioning Him privately, "Why could we not drive it out?"

29 And He said to them, "This kind cannot come out by anything but prayer."

Some translations say "prayer and fasting." (See also Matthew 17:19-21, though note that the NIV omits verse 21.) The purpose of fasting is to humble or chasten the soul (Psalm 35:13; Psalm 69:10).

Philippians 4:6-7

6 Do not be anxious about anything, but in everything, by prayer and petition, with thanksgiving, present your requests to God.

7 And the peace of God, which transcends all understanding, will guard your hearts and your minds in Christ Jesus.

Humility:

1 Chronicles 29:14-16

14 "But who am I, and who are my people, that we should be able to give as generously as this? Everything comes from you, and we have given you only what comes from your hand.

15 We are aliens and strangers in your sight, as were all our forefathers. Our days on earth are like a shadow, without hope.

16 O LORD our God, as for all this abundance that we have provided for building you a temple for your Holy Name, it comes from your hand, and all of it belongs to you.

Psalm 138:6

6 Though the LORD is on high, he looks upon the lowly, but the proud he knows from afar.

Obedience:

Psalm 37:4

4 Delight yourself in the LORD and he will give you the desires of your heart.

5 Commit your way to the LORD; trust in him and he will do this:

6 He will make your righteousness shine like the dawn, the justice of your cause like the noonday sun.

Praise:

Psalm 30:9-12

9 "What gain is there in my destruction, in my going down into the pit? Will the dust praise you? Will it proclaim your faithfulness?

10 Hear, O LORD, and be merciful to me; O LORD, be my help."

11 You turned my wailing into dancing; you removed my sackcloth and clothed me with joy,

12 that my heart may sing to you and not be silent. O LORD my God, I will give you thanks forever.

Praise indicates the inclination of the heart; serving to focus both us and others on the Lord.

Gratitude and Thanksgiving:

Deuteronomy 8:10-18

10 When you have eaten and are satisfied, praise the LORD your God for the good land he has given you.

11 Be careful that you do not forget the LORD your God, failing to observe his commands, his laws and his decrees that I am giving you this day.

12 Otherwise, when you eat and are satisfied, when you build fine houses and settle down,

13 and when your herds and flocks grow large and your silver and gold increase and all you have is multiplied,

14 then your heart will become proud and you will forget the LORD your God, who brought you out of Egypt, out of the land of slavery.

15 He led you through the vast and dreadful desert, that thirsty and waterless land, with its venomous snakes and scorpions. He brought you water out of hard rock.

16 He gave you manna to eat in the desert, something your fathers had never known, to humble and to test you so that in the end it might go well with you.

17 You may say to yourself, "My power and the strength of my hands have produced this wealth for me."

18 But remember the LORD your God, for it is he who gives you the ability to produce wealth, and so confirms his covenant, which he swore to your forefathers, as it is today.

Psalm 50:14-15

14 Sacrifice thank offerings to God, fulfill your vows to the Most High,

15 and call upon me in the day of trouble; I will deliver you, and you will honor me."

Psalm 116:12-14

12 How can I repay the LORD for all his goodness to me?

13 I will lift up the cup of salvation and call on the name of the LORD.

14 I will fulfill my vows to the LORD in the presence of all his people.

Gratitude is related to humility because we're giving credit where credit is truly due.

Hunger for God:

Jeremiah 29:12-13

12 Then you will call upon me and come and pray to me, and I will listen to you.

13 You will seek me and find me when you seek me with all your heart.

Matthew 7:8

8 For everyone who asks receives; he who seeks finds; and to him who knocks, the door will be opened.

What warnings are we given?

Regarding lingering sin and disobedience:

Judges 2:1-3

1 The angel of the LORD went up from Gilgal to Bokim and said, "I brought you up out of Egypt and led you into the land that I swore to give to your forefathers. I said, 'I will never break my covenant with you,

2 and you shall not make a covenant with the people of this land, but you shall break down their altars.' Yet you have disobeyed me. Why have you done this?

3 Now therefore I tell you that I will not drive them out before you; they will be [thorns] in your sides and their gods will be a snare to you."

Regarding motives and wholeheartedness:

1 Chronicles 28:9

9 "And you, my son Solomon, acknowledge the God of your father, and serve him with wholehearted devotion and with a willing mind, for the LORD searches every heart and understands every motive behind the thoughts. If you seek him, he will be found by you; but if you forsake him, he will reject you forever.

Regarding lack of commitment:

2 Chromicles 12:14

14 He did evil because he had not set his heart on seeking the LORD.

Regarding unrepented sin:

Psalm 66:18

18 If I had cherished sin in my heart, the Lord would not have listened;

Regarding motive:

Acts 8:18-24

18 When Simon saw that the Spirit was given at the laying on of the apostles' hands, he offered them money

19 and said, "Give me also this ability so that everyone on whom I lay my hands may receive the Holy Spirit."

20 Peter answered: "May your money perish with you, because you thought you could buy the gift of God with money!

21 You have no part or share in this ministry, because your heart is not right before God.

22 Repent of this wickedness and pray to the Lord. Perhaps he will forgive you for having such a thought in your heart.

23 For I see that you are full of bitterness and captive to sin."

24 Then Simon answered, "Pray to the Lord for me so that nothing you have said may happen to me."

When Christians are saved by faith in Christ, their sins are forgiven (see Romans 8:1-2) but the effect of sin is not entirely negated. Even Christians whose lifestyle is not in full alliance with the will of God can still be used by the Holy Spirit. But not only can their ministries be hindered dramatically and their witness compromised by lingering sin, but wrong motives and inconsistencies in their lives dishonor the Name of the Lord and hinder the work of the Church as a whole.

What reminders are we offered?

Ephesians 4:1-7

1 As a prisoner for the Lord, then, I urge you to live a life worthy of the calling you have received.

2 Be completely humble and gentle; be patient, bearing with one another in love.

3 Make every effort to keep the unity of the Spirit through the bond of peace.

4 There is one body and one Spirit—just as you were called to one hope when you were called—

5 one Lord, one faith, one baptism;

6 one God and Father of all, who is over all and through all and in all.

7 But to each one of us grace has been given as Christ apportioned it.

Chapter 3

ADMINISTRATION

———

Definition: The special ability to coordinate others by the guidance of the Holy Spirit to achieve a desired goal.

———

Scriptures cited in Chapter 3 – Administration

As a quality of God
Romans 8:28
Exodus 3:7-12

As illustrated in the Old Testament
Exodus 17:8-13
2 Samuel 11:2-17
1 Chronicles 21:1-7
2 Samuel 11:27-12:14
1 Chronicles 21:8-19
1 Chronicles 22:1-10
1Kings 5:12
1 Kings 6:15-36

As exemplified in Jesus' ministry
Matthew 28:18-20
Mark 3:13-15

As illustrated in the New Testament
Acts 6:1-7
Acts 14:23

Related teachings
Exodus 4:10-13
Exodus 4:14
Exodus 4:15-17
Exodus 1-8
Exodus 18:13-26
Exodus 18:20-23
Exodus 24:14
Mark 3:13
Matthew 10:1
Matthew 10:5-42

Exodus 17:11
Acts 7:35
1 Peter 2:13-14, 17
2 Samuel 12:1-9
Ephesians 4:11-16

Administration

> *Definition: The special ability to coordinate others by the guidance of the Holy Spirit to achieve a desired goal.*

As a quality of God

God is the Great Administrator—so great, in fact, that we are assured in Romans 8:28 that "in all things God works for the good of those who love him, who have been called according to his purpose." When we cooperate with His plans and allow Him to administer them and direct us as He sees fit, we who love Him will benefit.

In Exodus 3:7-12, it is clear that God was aware of His people's difficulties and He was concerned for their welfare. This is shown in the following steps: He responded (v. 8), He established His goal (v. 8), gave a directive to Moses (v. 10), and when Moses questioned him and sought clarification (v. 11), God used specifics to provide reassurance of ultimate success (v. 12). Notice that God said "*When* [not *if*] you have brought the people out, … you *will* [not *might*] worship *God* [assurance that they would recognize to whom they owe their worship] on *this* [not some undesignated] mountain."

As illustrated in the Old Testament

Moses also exercised the gift of administration. As we read in Exodus 17:8-13, Moses had a defined goal—to protect the Hebrew people. Toward that end he gave Joshua a clear directive (v. 9) while he himself took responsibility to hold the staff of God, representative of God's own presence and involvement, visible to encourage the Israelites (vv. 9-11). When the staff was raised, God was glorified; when it fell out of view, the warriors' focus seemed to turn from reliance on God to reliance on their own strength, and the battle turned against them (v. 11). Moses himself relied on the physical and psychological support that Aaron and

Hur provided (v. 12). This is a good example of how good coordination of a cooperative effort, directed by God and administered by Moses, helped to achieve their common goal.

Although King David is an example of a generally Godly king, he sometimes used his administrative power for selfish purposes (2 Samuel 11:2-17; 1 Chronicles 21:1-7). Such misuse always resulted in suffering (2 Samuel 11:27-12:14; 1 Chronicles 21:8-19). Although David recognized his sin before the consequences were entirely evident, God allowed the resulting consequences to bring David to full repentance—another sign of God's administering the overall sequence of events.

King David wanted to honor God by building a temple in Jerusalem (1 Chronicles 22:1-10). Despite all the evidence that this plan would meet with God's approval, it was not approved because it was not true to what David's life represented (v. 8). God assigned the task to Solomon instead (v. 9-10). Knowing that Solomon would be inexperienced in administration when he took on the task, David did use his own administrative position to make the task easier for his son to implement when the time came for Solomon to begin construction on the Temple (vv. 2-5). David also commissioned his son to carry out the task that God had delegated to Solomon, encouraging him by reiterating God's explanations and promises in that regard.

Solomon, too, demonstrated skill as a God-led administrator, in particular as he undertook construction of the Temple in Jerusalem, as recorded in chapters 5 and 6 of 1 Kings. He established his goals, evaluated his resources, contacted suppliers and negotiated for supplies, coordinated work among the Master Designer and craftsmen, and oversaw the construction through the project's completion. Notice that his administration was enhanced by his related God-given abilities, such as wisdom (1 Kings 5:12) and a sense of artistry (1 Kings 6:15-36).

As exemplified in Jesus' ministry

Jesus illustrated the gift of administration throughout His ministry. He had been given authority by God the Father (Matthew 28:18-20). He, in turn, appointed the twelve apostles with a three-fold purpose—to be companions to Him, to delegate specific tasks, and to extend His authority to them (Mark 3:13-15).

As illustrated in the New Testament

The gift of administration is illustrated in Acts 6:1-7, in which the twelve apostles were called upon to settle a dispute regarding distribution of food to the widows of the Greek Jews. The Twelve agreed that their primary responsibilities precluded their devoting their energy to this problem. They delegated authority to the local disciples (who were better acquainted with the men under consideration) to select seven overseers. The Twelve retained their authority, however, by specifying the criteria by which the selection should be made. The local church chose the delegates, whom the Twelve then commissioned by prayer and the laying on of hands.

Acts 14:23 records that, in a similar way, throughout their missionary journey, "Paul and Barnabas appointed elders for each church and, with prayer and fasting, committed them to the Lord, in whom they had put their trust."

Related teachings

Although questions seeking clarification and reassurance can be helpful to the administrator, who can then arrange for any support that may be required, questions challenging method or purpose are not appropriate. In Exodus 4:10-13 Moses questioned God's reasoning in choosing him and asked that someone else be called to do the job in his place. God was angered by this direct flouting of His administration and by Moses' reluctance to trust and obey (Exodus 4:14). Yet He demonstrated qualities of love, patience, kindness, gentleness, self-control, purpose, and flexibility (Exodus 4:15-17)—that allowed Him to maintain a good working relationship with Moses. Despite the barriers and objections that Moses presented to Him, God's ultimate goal was achieved.

It should be noted that the Hebrews' progress through the wilderness did not go as smoothly or as problem-free as it might have if Moses had agreed to God's original plan (Exodus 1-8). As a concessional member of the team, Aaron became, in the Hebrews' minds, a substitute for Moses, and the people began to rely on him rather than on their real leader. Whereas Moses was directly led by God, Aaron was only indirectly led by Him so was an unreliable authority.

Even Moses had to learn that administration involved appropriate delegation of authority. In Exodus 18:13-26 we read that Moses humbled himself to listen to Godly counsel from Jethro. He recognized the wisdom of delegating authority so that he was freed to spend his time and energy in the tasks that no one else was qualified to handle (vv. 24-26).

God taught Moses what he needed to know to accomplish his delegated responsibilities, one of which was to train others so that they would be qualified to do the tasks Moses assigned to them (Exodus 18:20-23).

In the same way that administration requires delegating authority, it also requires redirecting those under authority to recognize a deputy. In Exodus 24:14 Moses made clear to the elders—representatives of all the people under his authority—that Aaron and Hur had been delegated and given authority to judge among the people. The chain of authority needs to be recognized and observed. Each level is answerable to the higher authority and, ultimately, to God.

Notice that when Jesus selected "those He wanted" it was from among those followers who had already responded to Jesus' initial call (Mark 3:13). They might not have known what they were getting into, nor were they sure they would be willing to do whatever He wanted them for; but they were *willing* to be willing to do whatever He asked. He appointed them to a specific role and (eventually, when He had prepared them) told them what He expected of them. He also expected those under His authority (specifically, demons) to recognize the authority He had delegated to the Twelve.

As we see in Matthew 10:1 and 10:5-42, Jesus' administration included training the Twelve to use the authority He had given them, warning them about the difficulties and persecutions they would encounter, and assuring them of the reward that would await them for faithful service. In this way He was coordinating them to work as a team that would be responsive to the guidance of the Holy Spirit.

Those believers exercising the gift of administration are not the only people who were responsible to see that it is used effectively. In Exodus 17:11 we read that Moses was unable to hold his hands steady by himself. He needed support from Aaron and Hur. And he needed Joshua in the field with the fighting men. Even a person with a strong gift of administration cannot accomplish the entire task himself. Support of the administrator is essential. Not everyone will provide the same kind of support, but all are necessary.

As Acts 7:35 points out, no matter how they have come to recognize their call, those with the Spiritual gift of administration have been commissioned by God. Their authority is from Him, so opposing their administration is opposing God's authority. 1 Peter 2:13-14 and verse 17 reminds us of our responsibility to submit, for the Lord's sake, to every authority instituted among men. We are to show proper respect to everyone. (This is not to say, however, that abuse of authority should not be questioned, but anyone questioning authority must be careful that they are exercising *Spiritual* discernment as Nathan did when he confronted King David about his sin in 2 Samuel 12:1-9. Rather than relying on his own judgment, he received insight from the Lord.)

God gave us gifts to prepare His people for works of service, to help them mature in their understanding of and similarity to Christ, to build up the body of Christ so that it can do the work God intends for it to accomplish (Ephesians 4:11-16). Just as administrators are expected to serve faithfully as God has directed and empowered them, those under the administration are also responsible to support, assist, obey, and pray for the administrators. When everyone works in this way toward the same goal, they can more readily achieve God-intended success.

Chapter 4

APOSTLE

Definition: The special ability to successfully establish a church and oversee its administration

---

List of scriptures cited in Chapter 4 – Apostle

As a quality of God
Genesis 2:15-25
Revelation 2:7
Genesis 3:8
Genesis 3:11

As illustrated in the Old Testament
Genesis 6:5-8
Genesis 6:13-14
Genesis 6:19
Genesis 6:22
Genesis. 7:1; 7:23
Genesis 8:20-22
Genesis 9:1, 11, 16
Genesis 8:21
Genesis 12:1-5
Exodus 19:4-6
Exodus 20:2-7
Exodus 20:8-17
Exodus 20:18-20

As exemplified in Jesus' ministry
Hebrews 3:1-2
Matthew 10:1
Matthew 10:5-8
Matthew 10:11-16
Matthew 6:12

As illustrated in the New Testament
Acts 6:1-7
Acts 15:5-6
Acts 16:4
Acts 16:5

Related teachings
Hebrews 3:1-2
1 Thessalonians 5:12-13
1 Thessalonians 5:19-22
Matthew 10:12-15
1 Timothy 2:1-4
2 Corinthians 11:3-6
2 Corinthians 12:12
2 Corinthians 12:18-19
1 Thessalonians 2:5-12

Chapter 4
Apostle

*Definition: The special ability to successfully establish
a church and oversee its administration*

As a quality of God

God established the Church body when He created man to assist him
in caring for His creation. God provided Adam a companion suited
to his needs. They were pure and innocent, with no knowledge of evil.
God gave them full access to the Garden, including the tree of life, with
only one restriction—to never eat from the tree of knowledge of good
and evil (Genesis 2:15-25).

But as we read in the third chapter of Genesis, both Adam and Eve
succumbed to temptation to test the truth of God's word. Because they
had separated themselves from God spiritually through disobedience,
God physically separated them from His presence and His blessing
of intimacy with Him. And they no longer had access to the tree
of eternal life. Although He loved them, they were cursed with the
consequences of their disobedience. (But notice that the promise of
restoration appears in Revelation 2:7.)

From Adam and Eve, down through the generations, God has
continued to guide, direct, correct, discipline, protect, encourage,
and teach the truly universal body of His creation. All humanity is
incorporated in that Church, but not all people recognize Him as
God. Those who do not must remain spiritually separated from Him.
Of those who do recognize Him as God, not all acknowledge Him as
their sole Authority.

Yet He continues to seek them out, much as He called "Where are
you?" to Adam, who had hidden himself in the Garden (Genesis 3:8).
He knows where we are, but He wants to make us aware of our self-
imposed distance from Him and the reason behind it (Genesis 3:11).

As illustrated in the Old Testament

Through the generations, people continued to sin to such an extent that God dissolved and re-established the foundations of His universal Church through the faith of one man, Noah (Genesis 6:5-8). A lone man of faith would be the remnant from which God would reestablish a Godly nation (Genesis 6:13-14) and preserve the world's animal population (Genesis 6:19). Noah was obedient (Genesis 6:22), and God did what He said He would do (Genesis 7:1; 7:23). Noah responded with worship and gratitude for God's faithfulness; and God made a covenant with Him (Genesis 8:20-22; 9:1, 11, 16). Although God recognized humanity's sinful nature (Genesis 8:21), He remained faithful to us.

Many generations later, God again chose one man, Abram, from among a nation who worshiped false gods (Genesis 12:1-5). As He had with Noah, God made a covenant with Abram, who did honor Him as God. Through Abram, whom God renamed "Abraham," God established another Church body—the Nation of Israel—called out to be people faithful to His authority and blessed by a unique and ongoing relationship with Him.

Generations later, God, in the role of Apostle, again selected one man, Moses, to refine, teach, and strengthen His people, His Church (Exodus 19:4-6). Through Moses, He led them from a land of false gods and depravity toward a place where they could recognize His sovereignty and be blessed by a continuing relationship with Him.

God instilled in the people an understanding of His authority (Exodus 20:2-7). Only then did He present His requirements for and limits upon how His people were to behave (Exodus 20:8-17). Yet His authority and laws were not enough to bring the people into communion with Him. They were terrified to face Him without an intermediary (Exodus 20:18-20). Moses had to assure them that fear of God was preventive, to help them establish and maintain a healthy relationship with Him.

The Nation of Israel acknowledged God's authority, was guided by His laws, learned from His discipline, and grew proud in their unique relationship with Him—so proud that many placed their faith not in God but in their own self-righteousness. And they continued to sin.

As exemplified in Jesus' ministry

Although Jesus was the fulfillment of all the preceding Messianic prophecies, He did not meet the worldly expectations of the Jews of His day. So, for the most part, His claim as the long-awaited Messiah was dismissed. Among those who did recognize His authority as the Son of God, He established yet another Church body, this one founded on the new covenant—that of forgiveness through faith, by the blood of His sacrificial death.

Jesus was the Great Apostle (Hebrews 3:1-2). He designated the twelve chosen disciples as apostles, and vested them with authority to accomplish their tasks (Matthew 10:1). Much as God had done for Moses, Jesus provided specific instructions about the ministry His chosen disciples were to perform. He then proceeded to train them both through verbal instruction and through experience (Matthew 10:5-8). He also instructed them to be alert and responsive to their reception by those among whom they would minister (Matthew 10:11-16).

Later, when the risen Christ presented Himself to the disciples, He assured them that He was passing on to them the commission He had received from the Father. By telling them to "receive" the Holy Spirit, He was telling them that the Spirit would be available to them, but they must take responsibility for using the Spirit's empowerment.

And finally, He revealed to them the solemnity of their responsibility. What unfathomable power they wielded in the forgiveness—or not—of sins! It recalls to us His teaching from Matthew 6:12, "Forgive us our debts, as we also have forgiven our debtors." The measure of grace we use will be returned to us.

Before ascending into heaven, Jesus reminded His disciples of His authority, His commission of them, their own authority and empowerment, and their mission. He assured them that He would continue to oversee their lives and ministry.

As illustrated in the New Testament

The apostles did as they had been taught, teaching, preaching, laying on hands, interceding in prayer, healing, casting out demons, raising the dead, providing guidance and correction for the local churches they were establishing. They monitored the churches' progress and problems, providing guidance and encouragement as needed. But Acts 6:1-7 indicates that they also knew it was important to remain true to their calling and not be sidetracked by peripheral responsibilities for which others are better qualified.

When questionable teachings arose, the apostles met to identify errors and correct them (Acts 15:5-6), and to issue clarification of the matters in question (Acts 16:4). As reported in Acts 16:5, "the churches were strengthened in the faith and grew daily in numbers."

Related teachings

All believers have the responsibility to pay attention to the apostle in authority over them, just as Jesus was obedient to the Father, who was over Him (Hebrews 3:1-2; 1 Thessalonians 5:12-13). All believers are responsible to remain faithful to the teachings of the true gospel (1 Thessalonians 5:19-22).

Jesus taught the apostles that if a household is welcoming and responsive to an apostle, it would be blessed (Matthew 10:12-15); if not, the apostles were to waste no time or energy there.

Paul's first letter to Timothy (1Timothy 2:1-4), urged believers to pray for all those in authority... "that we may live peaceful and quiet lives in all godliness and holiness." Not only do all in authority benefit from God's guidance, but it is to our benefit to pray for that help.

It behooves all believers, however, to discern truth from deception and the true gospel from "different gospels," of which Paul wrote in 2 Corinthians 11:3-6. Verses 12-15 warn that believers must be able to identify counterfeit apostles. Even Satan himself can masquerade as an angel of light. So we must be able to recognize his deceptions.

Sincerity and devotion to Christ do not protect us entirely from deceptive teaching. We must be well founded in the truth so that we can recognize and shun distortions by those who "teach a different Jesus." In this way we will also be able to differentiate between true and false apostles.

Watch for signs, wonders, and miracles (2 Corinthians 12:12) that glorify God, not the apostle, and that strengthen the Church and do not exploit it (see 2 Corinthians 12:18-19). This is God's verification of an apostle's authenticity. A true apostle has no secret agenda; his primary purpose is to build up God's Church (1 Thessalonians 2:5-12), whose purpose, in turn, is to bring glory to God.

Chapter 5

LEADERSHIP

Definition: The special ability to motivate others by setting an example for them

---

Scriptures cited in Chapter 5 – Leadership

As a quality of God
Exodus 13:17-22
Numbers 6:22-27

As illustrated in the Old Testament
Numbers 27:15-23
Judges 6:15
Judges 6:12-17, 34-40
Judges 7:17-21
1 Samuel 18:12-17
1 Kings 15:25-26
Daniel 2:21
2 Kings 23:1-3

As exemplified in Jesus' ministry
John 13:12-17
John 13:34-35
John 14:31
Matthew 6:9-13

As illustrated in the New Testament
Acts 27:33-36
I Peter 5:8-11
Acts 1:15-26
1 Corinthians 8:9
2 Corinthians 1:12

Related teachings
1 Samuel 8:6-7
Proverbs 13:20
Ephesians 5:1-2
1 Samuel 12:23
Hebrews 12:2-3
Hebrews 13:7-8
Hebrews 13:17-18

Leadership

> *Definition: The special ability to motivate others by setting an example for them*

As a quality of God

When God delivered His people from slavery in the land of Egypt, He did not leave them to find their own way (Exodus 13:17-22). Instead, He assured the people of His presence. He went ahead of them all the way, day and night. He gave them a visible assurance of His presence that they could keep in sight.

God's leadership also involved decision making based on His knowledge of those whom He led. He chose the longer, more arduous route that would provide opportunity for them to develop their faith in His leadership rather than the route that would weaken their resolve (Exodus 13:17-18).

God also provided leadership to Aaron and to his sons, providing a specific instruction and example regarding how to invoke the name of the Lord to bless the sons of Israel (Numbers 6:22-27).

As illustrated in the Old Testament

Before Moses died, he asked God to provide another leader for the people. God designated Joshua to receive a portion of Moses' leadership authority. Yet Joshua remained under Moses' authority as long as Moses lived. Unlike Moses, who heard directly from God, Joshua was to obtain decisions from the Lord through the priest. Joshua was acknowledged publicly so the people would recognize his newly vested authority. Hands were laid on him, indicating God's blessing and approval; and he was commissioned, having his responsibility to the people clearly set out before them all so everyone knew what they could and should expect of him (Numbers 27:15-23).

When called into leadership, Gideon, in Judges 6:15, pointed out that he was the least likely selection for such a role. He sought assurance beyond question that it was the Lord's directions he was following and that he would have God's support on the mission. If we are to succeed in leadership, we must be sure of the Lord's direction to us before we ever attempt to direct others (Judges 6:12-17, 34-40).

Gideon told the soldiers under his authority what to do and to watch him and follow his lead as they charged the enemy camp (Judges 7:17-21). As leaders, we must be willing to place ourselves on the frontlines. If we stay to the rear, those who follow us will be going in the wrong direction and will accomplish nothing. In the front, however, a leader can set an example and provides encouragement and direction for those who follow.

As we see in 1 Samuel 18:12-17, when God is directing a leader, the undertaking will be successful. We do well to remember, however, that remarkable success can create envy and fear in those who perceive themselves as threatened by the leadership.

There is a difference between God-ordained leadership and God-directed leadership. God may ordain or anoint a leader, but unless that leader seeks and obeys God's guidance, the leader is not God-directed. As we see in 1 Kings 15:25-26, although Nadab had been established by God as king of Israel (Daniel 2:21) he did not follow God's precepts. He did evil and caused his nation to sin. In God-directed leadership, however, authority is used for God's glory (2 Kings 23:1-3).

As exemplified in Jesus' ministry

Jesus set the example of humbling Himself in service to others as He washed His disciples' feet, leading the way for His disciples to follow (John 13:12-17). He also set the example in unreservedly loving others (John 13:34-35) and in obedience to the Father (John 14:31). He led his disciples not only physically, from place to place, but by example, showing them how to rely fully on the Father and how to effectively minister to the desperate people they encountered daily.

Much as God had set an example for Aaron of how to invoke His blessing on the sons of Israel, Jesus led His disciples by providing a template, which we refer to as the Lord's prayer (Matthew 6:9-13), to teach them how to approach the Father in prayer.

As illustrated in the New Testament

In Acts 27:33-36, we see the Apostle Paul taking a leadership role despite his status as prisoner. The ship had been storm battered for two solid weeks, so that neither passengers nor seasoned crew were able to eat anything. Although he was a Roman prisoner on the ship, Paul stepped into a leadership role. He knew that everyone onboard faced imminent shipwreck and that their survival would depend on their regaining their strength. He encouraged the others to eat, and he set the example for them by eating some himself. By this they were encouraged, and, eating, they soon regained enough strength to survive the shipwreck.

1 Peter 5:8-11 encourages all of us to be example-setting leaders for others in situations similar to our own, despite Satan's attempts to dissuade us or cause us to compromise our integrity.

Those who are called into leadership must remain faithful, or, like Judas, they will be removed from office and their place filled with someone else who will serve faithfully (Acts 1:15-26).

Despite our freedom in Christ, we are warned to avoid becoming a stumbling block to those weaker than we who may be following our example (1 Corinthians 8:9). Rather than exercising our freedoms to others' detriment, we are to conduct ourselves in all situations, including among people under our leadership, with a Godly sincerity and purity of purpose (2 Corinthians 1:12).

Related teachings

1 Samuel 8:6-7 reminds us that rejection of a God-appointed leader is rejection of God's own leadership. We must be careful of whose leadership we choose to follow (Proverbs 13:20).

As Christians, we are expected to follow Christ's leadership and example of living in love and willing sacrifice (Ephesians 5:1-2). Whether we are leaders or followers, we are expected to pray for those in authority over us and continue to teach and encourage others to lead with integrity (1 Samuel 12:23).

We are admonished in Hebrews 12:2-3 to consider Christ's goal and what He was willing to suffer for the sake of achieving that goal. As His followers, we should remain as focused and committed through the encouragement of His example. Jesus doesn't change over the years or under varied circumstances. The goal and His faithfulness to His followers remain the same.

Hebrews 13:7-8 encourages us to follow the examples of those Christians who preceded us in faith, those who followed Jesus' example of faithfulness and sacrifice. We are to follow those who are placed in positions of leadership over us. The heavier the burden we place on our leaders, the more difficult their task becomes and the less effectively they can work. On the other hand, if we ease their burden, seeking God's help in reaching His goals for them, our leaders will become more efficient and effective. It is difficult to lead when no one will follow. But the burden of leadership is lightened when followers willingly submit to their authority and support their leaders with prayer (Hebrews 13:17-18).

Chapter 6

EVANGELISM

Definition: The special ability to express the gospel in such a way that people know the conviction of the Holy Spirit, repent, and seek salvation.

Scriptures cited in Chapter 6 – Evangelism

As a quality of God
Exodus 3:2-6
Exodus 3:11-22
Exodus 4:1-31
1 Samuel 3:1-21
2 Chronicles 34:15-27

As illustrated in the Old Testament
Isaiah 1:2, 16-17
Jonah 1:1-3
Jonah 4:5-10

As exemplified in Jesus' ministry
Matthew 4:23-25
Matthew 9:35-38
Luke 19:1-10
John 4:7-26
John 4:39-42
Luke 4:43-44
Luke 9:1-2

As illustrated in the New Testament
Acts 2:14-41
Acts 8:4
Acts 9:17-22
Acts 13:26
Acts 14:1-3

Related teachings
Acts 18:5-8
Acts 19:8-10
Acts 26:20
Acts 24:24-25
2 Corinthians 5:20
1 Corinthians 1:17
2 Corinthians 4:1-7
1 Corinthians 9:11-14

Chapter 6
Evangelism

> *Definition: The special ability to express the gospel in such a way that people know the conviction of the Holy Spirit, repent, and seek salvation.*

As a quality of God

When God revealed Himself to Moses (Exodus 3:2-6), in effect evangelizing him, Moses acknowledged both God's supremacy and his own deep sense of unworthiness.

But God provided assurance (Exodus 3:11-22) that Moses was, indeed, God's choice and would have His support in what he had been called to do. God also assured him that his message would be believed, not by fluent speech but through the demonstration of God's power (Exodus 4:1-31). God convicted Moses, yet Moses was hesitant to obey, to accept his role in the salvation God offered. He needed further convincing. God answered his questions and silenced Moses' doubts by incorporating miracles—signs and wonders—to provide the needed assurance. Even when God is angry with us, He addresses our concerns to offer a compromise. But with God, some things are non-negotiable.

God also revealed Himself to Samuel (1 Samuel 3:1-21) to prepare him for his prophetic role. By Samuel's speaking to Eli concerning the Lord's message, Eli was convicted and accepted the consequences of his sin, although without any apparent expression of repentance. But through the experience, Samuel came to respect and honor the truth of God's word.

God spoke pointedly to Josiah through His Word (2 Chronicles 34:15-27). Notice, in particular, verse 27, "because your heart was responsive and you humbled yourself before God... I have heard you, declares the Lord."

As illustrated in the Old Testament

Evangelism in the Old Testament often appears in the form of words of admonishment, knowledge, or prophecy to assure individuals of God's concern and involvement in their lives. The purpose appears to have been to draw them into a closer, more trusting relationship with Him (Isaiah 1:2, 16-17).

Unlike the preceding examples, in which individuals had been obedient and responded positively to God's call to know Him more closely, when Jonah was directed to prophesy against Ninevah, he ran from God (Jonah 1:1-3). Therefore, God needed stronger methods to obtain Jonah's compliance. Jonah finally, and unwillingly, obeyed and was dismayed when the people of Ninevah repented. God can prosper His purposes for salvation even when our attitude is less forgiving...but, like Jonah, we suffer the consequences of our own lack of compassion (Jonah 4:5-10).

As exemplified in Jesus' ministry

Jesus combined preaching and healing to attract an audience whom He could teach (Matthew 4:23-25). He had compassion on the crowds who responded, knowing that, beyond His initial teaching, they would need continuing guidance (Matthew 9:35-38).

He identified and responded to individuals who sought Him out. Zacchaeus began with a simple curiosity about who Jesus was (Luke 19:1-10), but Jesus' personal acknowledgement of him and urgent response to his needs led this reputed sinner to repent, offer restitution, and be saved.

Jesus also sought out individuals through whom He could reach others. When He spoke with a Samaritan woman drawing water, He used the water as a conversation starter to introduce the gospel message and Himself (John 4:7-26). Her testimony back in the town caused many to believe in Him and seek Him out for themselves (John 4:39-42).

But as an evangelist, Jesus could not stay in one location to follow up with a single group (Luke 4:43-44), so He trained select disciples to fill the needed support roles to extend the reach of His ministry (Luke 9:1-2).

As illustrated in the New Testament

Peter's first sermon (Acts 2:14-41), by the power of the Holy Spirit, was extraordinarily successful. Make special note of verse 37, in which his listeners were "cut to the heart"—convicted—and sought the way to salvation. "...About three thousand were added to their number that day."

Those disciples who had been scattered, due to persecution (Acts 8:4), were empowered to preach the Word wherever they went.

Although Saul was well known as a persecutor of Christians, he was transformed on the road to Damascus by his encounter with the risen Christ. In Acts 9:17-22, Saul appears to have been simultaneously healed of both his physical and spiritual blindness. He was anointed as an evangelist and turned from persecuting believers to spreading the good news of the gospel. Notice that after regaining his physical strength and spending time in fellowship with the brethren, he began using his gift "at once."

Acts 13:26 tells us that the good news is available to all God-fearing people, no matter what their cultural background may be.

God can confirm the validity of the gospel message through signs and wonders, as He did in Acts 14:1-3.

Related teachings

So long as evangelists testify as the Holy Spirit directs, if the message is ignored, the responsibility is no longer on the evangelist; consequences for unbelief then fall on the shoulders of the non-believers (Acts 18:5-8). The evangelist is free to redirect his efforts to more willing recipients (Acts 19:8-10).

The evangelist's message (Acts 26:20) includes the need for repentance and turning to God, as well as a change of behavior to indicate a true change of heart. But, despite a listener's interest, conviction doesn't always lead to repentance (Acts 24:24-25). The overriding message of the evangelist is to "Be reconciled to God" (2 Corinthians 5:20).

Each believer is given a specific purpose (1 Corinthians 1:17) directed and inspired by the Holy Spirit, who knows both our hearts and the hearts of our hearers—a more complete and more trustworthy guide than the natural mind, which is limited in its knowledge and understanding. This is especially important in evangelism because without the Holy Spirit we can't discern the motivations and conditions of our listeners' hearts.

Paul indicated in 2 Corinthians 4:1-7 that he was encouraged to pursue his ministry because he knew that it was God's will to enlighten the hearts of men, despite Satan's attempt to blind people unwilling to accept the truth. It was the very fallibility of Paul's humanity (his "jar of clay") that proved that the power of the gospel is from God and not from man.

1 Corinthians 9:11-14 tells us that those pastors, preachers, and evangelists who work to build up the Church should be able to expect financial and material support for their efforts.

Chapter 7

PASTORING

---

*Definition: The special ability to guide individuals
in the development of their relationship with
the Lord over an extended period of time.*

Scriptures cited in Chapter 7 – Pastoring

As a quality of God
Psalm 23:1-3
2 Chronicles 15:1-2

As illustrated in the Old Testament
Exodus, chs. 16-17
Exodus 33:12-23
Exodus 18:17-27
Numbers 11:11-17
Psalm 78:70-72

As exemplified in Jesus' ministry
Matthew 3:16-17
Matthew 4:1-11
Mark 1:14-2:13
John 21:15-17

As illustrated in the New Testament
Acts 2:38-42
Acts 10
Acts 10:25-26
Acts 15:6-11
1 Peter 1-4
1 Timothy 1:18;
1 Timothy 2:1-3;
2 Timothy 4:2-6
2 Timothy 1:6-7;
2 Timothy 3:12-17

Related teachings
Acts 20:28-31
2 Timothy 3:1-5
Jeremiah 23:1-4
Ezekiel 34:1-16

Zechariah 11:17
1 Corinthians 9:11-14
Matthew 5:44
Luke 18:1
Luke 22:32
1 Thessalonians 5:17-18, 25
James 5:19-20
Deuteronomy 33:1, 8-11

Pastoring

> *Definition: The special ability to guide individuals in the development of their relationship with the Lord over an extended period of time.*

As a quality of God

One of the clearest descriptions of God's characteristics as a pastor appears in Psalm 23:1-3. God sees to all our physical and emotional needs, providing us with opportunities for rest and refreshment, healing, encouragement, protection, guidance, and purpose.

He keeps track of each individual, watching and protecting us from danger, seeking us out if we wander off on our own and can't find our own way back (2 Chronicles 15:1-2). Despite His faithful and willing concern for our wellbeing, if we choose to forsake Him, intentionally turning away and hiding from Him, He won't hunt us down or force us to return to Him.

As illustrated in the Old Testament

Just as God called Moses to lead His people from Egypt to the Promised Land, He delegates all human pastors as "under-shepherds," subject to His direction. He guides and teaches his commissioned pastors regarding where and how to guide others. Pastoring in the Old Testament took many forms.

The book of Exodus illustrates Moses as physically leading the "flock" of Hebrews through the wilderness, protecting them, providing for their physical needs (Exodus chs. 16-17), teaching and rebuking or encouraging them when they were disobedient or discouraged— all according to direct guidance from God to Moses himself. As Moses acknowledged his dependence on God's guidance, God met his needs (Exodus 33:12-23) but with protective limitations. When Moses disobeyed, misunderstood, or needed correction, God corrected, encouraged, and strengthened his faith to continue. Through Jethro, God revealed to him the benefit of delegating responsibility to others to share the burden of the tasks before him (Exodus 18:17-27), which indicates that God provides pastoral care and guidance for the "shepherd" as well as the "flock."

When Moses acknowledged that he couldn't carry the entire load of responsibility for the people himself, God directed him to delegate others to assist him. God empowered those helpers to fulfill the tasks to which they were called (Numbers 11:11-17).

God also called David from literally shepherding sheep (Psalm 78:70-72) to pastoring Israel from the throne, commissioning him to specific increasing responsibilities, step by step, similarly guiding, protecting, and correcting, and by teaching David through consequences for sin and disobedience. Through God's guidance, David also learned to delegate work to others and to discern Godly from ungodly counsel.

As exemplified in Jesus' ministry

Jesus, too, was prepared by God for pastoring others. Immediately following His baptism and affirmation from God (Matthew 3:16-17), God's Spirit led Him into the wilderness (Matthew 4:1-11). Although we might see this as leading Him into temptation, God used this confrontation with the devil to reinforce Jesus' already-firm resolve and commitment before beginning His public ministry.

Jesus' pastorate grew as He learned. Beginning with teaching with authority, healings, and exorcism of unclean spirits (Mark 1:14-2:13), He selected disciples—those whom He would pastor personally. He shepherded them continuously through teaching, encouraging, guiding, counseling, correcting, and—most importantly—by His own example of continually seeking God's direction. He would eventually delegate these men to extend His ministry by commissioning them to continue the work when He could no longer be physically present.

When Jesus commissioned Peter (John 21:15-17), His direction to "Feed my lambs," suggests that even the newest, most naïve of believers were to be encouraged and provided nourishment to increase their understanding and faith. The second part of the commission, "Take care of my sheep," suggested that pastoring was an ongoing process requiring continuing, wide-ranging diligence. Although Peter's feelings were hurt by the repetitiveness of the inquiries, Jesus was patiently emphasizing the need to stay in touch with the pastor's purpose and resolve in seeing the commission through to fruition, and continuing to provide spiritual sustenance even for mature believers.

As illustrated in the New Testament

Peter was called to minister to both Jews and Gentiles (Acts 2:38-42; Acts 10). He provided humble correction to misguided individuals (Acts 10:25-26) and guidance to the other apostles (Acts 15:6-11; 1 Peter 1-4). In this regard, his pastoral role overlapped with his role as an apostle.

Although Paul, as a missionary, rarely remained in any city for very long, he did pastor numerous churches through his written correspondence and by his personal example of committed service. This gift also overlapped with his role as apostle. When his message was rejected by local authorities, he moved on but remained in touch with the local community of believers to offer ongoing encouragement, guidance, and correction through his letters to the various church communities he had visited on his missionary journeys.

Paul also personally pastored Timothy, teaching (1 Timothy 1:18; 1 Timothy 2:1-3; 2 Timothy 4:2-6) and encouraging him (2 Timothy 1:6-7; 2 Timothy 3:12-17) much as a father would, to train him for Timothy's own ministry.

Related teachings

Pastors must be alert to those who might try to mislead the people, recognizing and counteracting strong, selfish, and ungodly influences that will attempt to entice people away from God (Acts 20:28-31; 2 Timothy 3:1-5).

Pastors who are unfaithful to their calling (Jeremiah 23:1-4; Ezekiel 34:1-16; Zechariah 11:17) will be held accountable by God. Though 1 Corinthians 9:11-14 tells us that pastors, preachers, and evangelists whose efforts go toward building up the Church should be able to expect financial and material support for their work, the work should be undertaken from a sincere desire to serve, not for financial gain.

Pastors and flock alike need to pray continually for one another (Matthew 5:44; Luke 18:1; Luke 22:32; 1 Thessalonians 5:17-18, 25), encouraging and affirming one another in their good work (James 5:19-20).

We should pray for our pastors, much as Moses did (Deuteronomy 33:1, 8-11), that they will teach God's ways, preach the gospel, honor God, and know His blessing and protection.

Chapter 8

TEACHING

Definition: The special ability to disseminate information in such a way that it is readily and clearly understood, with the purpose of building up the Church.

Scriptures cited in Chapter 8 – Teaching

As a quality of God
Exodus 12:1-21
Exodus 12:21-23

As illustrated in the Old Testament
Exodus 12:24-28
Nehemiah 8:7-8

As exemplified in Jesus' ministry
Luke 11:2-13
Matthew 7:28-29
John 7:16
John 7:16-18
John 14:22-24

As illustrated in the New Testament
Acts 8:26-38
Acts 17:2-4
Acts 17:10-12
Acts 17:16-23

Related teachings
Psalm 78:1-8
Proverbs 22:6
Proverbs 16:23
Proverbs16:21
Luke 6:39-45
Proverbs 22:12
Acts 17:10-12
2 Timothy 2:14-16
2 Timothy 2:23-25
Psalm 119:27
Proverbs 1:1-9
Proverbs 1:5

Proverbs 22:17-21
Proverbs 23:12
Hebrews 5:12-14
2 Timothy 2:2
Galatians 6:6
2 Timothy 3:16-17
Titus 2:1-15
James 3:1
Matthew 5:19

Chapter 8
Teaching

> *Definition: The special ability to disseminate information in such a way that it is readily and clearly understood, with the purpose of building up the Church.*

As a quality of God

God, as teacher, gave Moses and Aaron specific directions in Exodus 12:1-21 about what to do with the lamb and about bread made without yeast—who is to eat it, how and when it is to be eaten, and why—and anticipated other questions that would arise.

Then Moses, in turn, used God's pattern for teaching to teach the elders (Exodus 12:21-23), just as he had been taught by God. Notice that Moses had the elders act immediately on what they had learned, just as God had had Moses act immediately on what he had been taught. This helped solidify the lessons in their minds.

As illustrated in the Old Testament

God had taught Moses, who taught the elders, who taught the people, who were, in turn, to teach their children (Exodus 12:24-28), on down through the generations. In this single chapter, God Himself provided us a wonderful example of what teaching is all about.

Good teachers, like the Levites in Nehemiah 8:7-8, present the facts, make them understandable, and explain the meaning and purpose so that the listeners can appropriately and accurately apply the information.

As exemplified in Jesus' ministry

The entire passage of Luke 11:2-13, in which Jesus had been asked to teach His disciples how to pray, illustrates Jesus as the Master Teacher.

Notice how He also teaches us *how* to teach by providing [a] a pattern (vv. 1-4), [b] an example for comparison (vv. 5-8), [c] application (v. 9) and [d] the principles involved (v. 10). In this segment He has provided the pattern upon which we can base all our prayers. Finally (vv. 11-13) He gives another example of application and comparison to illuminate the principles.

Jesus taught through the use of parables, stories to which his listeners could relate. He spoke with authority (Matthew 7:28-29) because, unlike the teachers of the law, He was directed and empowered by the Holy Spirit (John 7:16).

Even Jesus relied on leading from the Holy Spirit. He does not ask us to believe in His teaching without confirming its truth first with the Holy Spirit (John 7:16-18). He points out in verse 18 that anyone sent by the Holy Spirit to teach will not be in it to bring glory to himself but to bring glory to God. This is one way to recognize false teachers and cult leaders.

Even Jesus recognized that not everyone would believe Him or obey His teaching, which is why He taught, as directed by the Holy Spirit, in such a way that His followers could understand but that was veiled from the understanding of non-believers (John 14:22-24).

As illustrated in the New Testament

The Ethiopian eunuch whom Philip encountered on the road to Gaza (Acts 8:26-38) recognized that he needed someone to explain what he was reading in the book of Isaiah; Philip explained the gospel in terms of the scripture before them in such a way that the Ethiopian understood and accepted Christ.

In Acts 17:2-4, Paul reasoned, explained, and proved to his listeners his gospel message. As in the preceding example, this was not evangelism but teaching, since the listeners were persuaded rather than convicted.

Good teaching should hold up under examination, as it did in Acts 17:10-12. The Bereans, though eagerly hearing the message, were wise to test Paul's teaching rather than accepting it blindly. Because they found it to be accurate, they could believe the gospel message he had presented.

Although Paul and the Athenians were of different cultures, he found a way to teach them by approaching them on the foundation of their own knowledge base (Acts 17:16-23). He made a connection that they could understand and that made them feel that he understood them. This approach overlaps the gifts of teaching and missions.

Related teachings

Psalm 78:1-8 tells us to pass on knowledge from generation to generation, including the warnings from what history has taught us regarding rebellion and being unfaithful to God. We should begin early to teach a child Godly precepts, which will remain available to him to guide him throughout his lifetime (Proverbs 22:6).

"A wise man's heart guides his mouth, and his lips promote instruction" (Proverbs 16:23); Proverbs 16:21 reinforces that theme by reminding us that "pleasant words promote instruction." It's easier to accept kind words of instruction or correction than harsh ones.

Teachers must take care to exhibit qualities as well as information they wish to teach (Luke 6:39-45). A student will be inclined to emulate his teacher's example in actions, attitudes, and behaviors, as well as learning from the spoken word. To be effective, a teacher's lifestyle must match his message (Proverbs 22:12).

A teacher's listeners should be expected to question what they hear in order to verify its truth, as the Bereans did in Acts 17:10-12. We are not to waste time and energy by arguing over semantics and meaningless issues. It detracts from lessons of value (2 Timothy 2:14-16). We are to avoid quarrels but be kind to everyone so we can gently instruct those who oppose us (2 Timothy 2:23-25) "in hope that God will grant them repentance leading them to a knowledge of the truth."

The purpose of seeking understanding is to grow in our relationship with God (Psalm 119:27).

Proverbs 1:1-9 offers a wealth of advice; "Let the wise listen and add to their learning" (Proverbs 1:5). "Pay attention and ... apply your heart to what I teach" (Proverbs 22:17-21).

"Apply your heart to instruction and your ears to words of knowledge" (Proverbs 23:12). To grow in maturity, we must apply what we learn (Hebrews 5:12-14). If called to do so by the Holy Spirit, we should also be able to teach others who will, in turn, teach others (2 Timothy 2:2).

The student who has benefitted from instruction needs to reciprocate, sharing "all good things with his instructor" (Galatians 6:6). This involves not only monetarily but with words of appreciation and enlightenment. In this way the teacher also benefits and is encouraged.

2 Timothy 3:16-17 teaches that scripture is a trustworthy resource to equip us for every good work. Titus 2:1-15 even provides a general curriculum for teaching.

However, James 3:1 should be taken as an alert to those who would take on teaching duties if the Holy Spirit does not call them to teach. They will be held accountable for whatever they teach. They will also be held accountable for living in accordance with whatever they teach. Teaching is an honorable calling but is not a responsibility to be taken lightly. (See also Matthew 5:19.)

Chapter 9

PROPHECY

Definition: The special ability to voice God's word, as revealed by the Holy Spirit to one, to be spoken aloud to others

---

Scriptures cited in Chapter 9 – Prophecy

As a quality of God
Exodus 4:10-17
Exodus 7:1-2
Jeremiah 1:4-19

As illustrated in the Old Testament
1 Kings 14: 1-18
2 Chronicles 11:1-4
2 Chronicles 12:5-8
2 Chronicles 15:1-8
Isaiah 44:24-26
Jeremiah 3:12-15

As exemplified in Jesus' ministry
Matthew 17:22-23
Matthew 26:34-35
Luke 4:24-27
John 12:49-50

As illustrated in the New Testament
Luke 2:29-35
Luke 2:26
Acts 13:1-5
Acts 13:7-12
Acts 15:32
Acts 27:10-26

Related teachings
2 Peter 1:20-21
Numbers 11:25-29
Numbers 12:5-9
Ezekiel 2:3-8
Ezekiel 12:1-6, 11
Numbers 12-13

2 Samuel 7:17
Deuteronomy 13:1-5
Proverbs 13:17
2 Kings 20:1-7
Ezekiel 13:1-9
2 Chronicles 18:9-22
Acts 1:16
Jeremiah 25:4-7
2 Chronicles 25:14-16
Deuteronomy 18:18-22
Jeremiah 26:2-3
Jeremiah 26:7-15
Jeremiah 26:16-19
Jeremiah 28:8-9
Jeremiah 3:12-15
Ezekiel 3:11, 18-19
Ezekiel 33:1-9
Ezekiel 33:30-33
Ezekiel 12:25-28
Jeremiah 29:18-19
Luke 4:24-27
Jonah 1:1-17
Matthew 7:15
Acts 16:16
Acts 2:30-31
Acts 10:43
1 Corinthians 13:2
1 Corinthians 14:1-5, 22-26
1 Corinthians 14:29-31, 39-40
1 Thessalonians 5:19-21
Revelation 19:10

Chapter 9
Prophecy

> *Definition: The special ability to voice God's word, as revealed by the Holy Spirit to one, to be spoken aloud to others*

As a quality of God

God spoke to Moses, as related in Exodus 4:10-17, teaching him how to be His prophet, foretelling what he would do and how it would be accomplished. When Moses demurred, God was patient and allowed Moses to share in the experience of having a substitute "mouth" through which he would speak. This allowed Moses to understand the need for cooperation in saying exactly what he would be told to say. God assured Moses that his messages would be verified by his miraculous use of the staff.

The role of Moses with Aaron as prophet (described in Exodus 7:1-2) is a substitutionary representative of God with Moses as prophet. In this way, Moses could better understand God's role and the importance of obeying God's directions as Moses shared God's word with others.

Jeremiah 1:4-19 indicates that God has a purpose for us even before we are born. He provides the anointing, the direction, the empowerment, and the encouragement we need. He provides a sense of purpose. Notice that the purposes of Jeremiah's prophetic gift are clearly stated (v. 10). God also provides the teaching and preparation we need to accomplish our calling (vv. 11-19). And He continues to encourage us as we need it, reminding us of our purpose and His help in accomplishing His goals.

As illustrated in the Old Testament

When we read 1 Kings 14:1-18, we see that prophecy is often used in conjunction with the gift of knowledge (v. 5). Old Testament prophecies often included a reminder of God's provision and kindness (vv. 7-8).

We see exhortation or admonishment in the recognition of sin and deception (v. 9), and a promise or warning of consequences.

We again see prophetic exhortation in 2 Chronicles 11:1-4, in which God used prophecy to correct misguided actions. And in 2 Chronicles 12:5-8, prophetic exhortation is used to warn of the consequences of unfaithfulness. This led to repentance and restoration. Notice that God reveals His purpose for allowing some consequences to remain (v. 8): "That they may learn…"

He used prophecy in 2 Chronicles 15:1-8 to reveal His conditions for relationship with Him, and to offer encouragement.

God shows us in Isaiah 44:24-26 that He undermines fallacy; but He fulfills the words and predictions of His own messengers because they speak His will.

The prophetic message, as shown in Jeremiah 3:12-15, often includes multiple parts: return, repent, be forgiven and restored, and be taught.

As exemplified in Jesus' ministry

Jesus' words of His imminent betrayal (Matthew 17:22-23) were intended not to cause grief but to provide foreknowledge and encouragement about what was to happen in the days ahead. Without trust in God's ultimate outcome for good, prophecy can be frightening and discouraging.

Jesus used prophecy to correct Peter's mistaken assumption in Matthew 26:34-35 that he was more committed than God actually knew him to be. Peter tried to deny the prophecy because he didn't want to believe that he could be fearful or weak enough to deny Christ. But God knows us better than we know ourselves; and He knows the future.

Jesus warned us in Luke 4:24-27 that not all prophets are called to all localities or in all circumstances. People are inclined to ignore prophecies given by others with whom they are acquainted, discounting their messages as being limited by human standards and understanding.

In general, the better we think we know individuals, the less likely we are to accept them as extraordinary vessels called for God's use, employed and anointed as mouth pieces for God.

Jesus tells us in John 12:49-50, that, even as God's own Son, He remained fully obedient to the Father's direction in what and how to speak. He did not rely on His human understanding of people and their circumstances when speaking. Because He knew that the goal of His omniscient Father was to benefit all, He relied on God's direction regarding what and how to speak in any situation.

As illustrated in the New Testament

The prophecy by Simeon (Luke 2:29-35), regarding Jesus' ultimate purpose and destiny, might also be considered a word of knowledge, since it could have been revealed to him only by the Holy Spirit (Luke 2:26).

We see in Acts 13:1-5 that not all prophets are called in the same way or to the same tasks. God calls us individually for specific purposes, much as Saul and Barnabas were singled out from among the other prophets and teachers of the church in Antioch. The personalities of the two men were quite different, but they complemented each other in a way that suited God's purposes for them.

Prophecy is sometimes accompanied by miracles, as it was in Acts 13:7-12, in which Saul confronted Elymas and prophesied his blindness in response to the magician's deceit. The fulfillment of that prophecy witnessed to the prophet's own legitimacy and veracity.

The purpose of prophecy referred to in Acts 15:32 appears to have been for encouragement and edification.

In Acts 27:10-26, the foreknowledge Paul spoke to discourage resuming the voyage from Fair Havens near Lasea, despite dangerous conditions, was ignored. The ship was placed in a life-threatening situation as a direct result of the officials' ignoring God's warning given through Paul's prophecy. Despite having been rejected and the prophecy ignored, Paul offered only a brief rebuke before resuming the prophecy of encouragement. His focus was on the encouragement rather than on the rebuke.

Related teachings

We are reminded in 2 Peter 1:20-21 that Scriptural prophecy is not derived from the human will but comes from those who spoke from God, as "moved by the Holy Spirit" (NASB).

The Holy Spirit was active in the Old Testament, as we read in Numbers 11:25-29, but did not abide in His people. His gifts were often for a limited time, for specific purposes. Today, as then, we are not to be jealous of the gifts when they are revealed, but we should rejoice that God can work in this way through His people.

God reveals Himself in various ways to His prophets, as indicated in Numbers 12:5-9. It angers Him to hear them criticized. God feeds the prophet, figuratively if not literally (as He did in Ezekiel 2:3-8) the words to speak to others. Sometimes the prophet is used as an example, a "sign" to the people, when words alone are not enough (Ezekiel 12:1-6, 11).

Prophets are to strictly follow the Lord's commands, as Balaam did (Numbers 12:12-13), and the prophecy given in its entirety, as Nathan did in 2 Samuel 7:17.

Deuteronomy 13:1-5 makes it clear that, as believers, we all have the responsibility to discern true, God-led prophets from counterfeits and others who would mislead God's people. The Lord hates counterfeit prophecy. The opportunity for relationship healing is one test of a God-ordained prophet. One who offers no opportunity for restoration is probably not speaking for the Lord (Proverbs 13:17). Godly prophecy provides an opportunity for repentance and forgiveness. As shown in 2 Kings 20:1-7, the Lord withdrew His judgment in response to Hezekiah's prayer.

Do not prophesy from your own imagination (Ezekiel 13:1-9). A true prophet of God will speak only the truth of what the Lord reveals to him. Although Micaiah spoke the words the king wanted to hear, as recorded in 2 Chronicles 18:9-22, he said them in such a way that the king recognized that they were false. If a listener insists on hearing only "prophecies" they want to hear, they are likely to be enticed and misled by falsehoods. Though fulfillment of the prophecy is not always immediate, the truth of prophecy is revealed by its fulfillment (Acts 1:16).

The result of the wrong choice of response, ignoring God's warnings, is illustrated in Jeremiah 25:4-7. By continuing to provoke God, the people brought the resulting harm upon themselves. It is always unwise to reject God's counsel, and especially so when He has sent it as a warning that offers the opportunity for repentance, as we see in 2 Chronicles 25:14-16. He calls to account those who do not respond to a prophet called by God, who speaks in His name (Deuteronomy 18:18-22).

The priests and false prophets offered the wrong response to God's rebuke and to Jeremiah because of the prophecy given in Jeremiah 26:2-3. They would bear the guilt for rejecting Jeremiah's prophecy on behalf of the entire city (Jeremiah 26:7-15). When the people discerned the truth, they spoke up (Jeremiah 26:16-19), correcting their leaders' rejection of the prophecy. This was an appropriate response in support of God's prophet.

Many would-be prophets gain popularity by saying what their audience wants to hear. Although God's prophecy often includes encouragements, in order to bring reconciliation between God and man it usually also involves warnings, corrections, and other elements that the public does not want to hear. Therefore, we are warned to be leery of purely positive prophecy and to test it carefully before accepting it as being from God (Jeremiah 28:8-9).

The prophetic message, as exemplified in Jeremiah 3:12-15, often includes multiple parts: return, repent, be forgiven and restored, and be taught. Those who have been called to prophesy should take their calling seriously. Notice that if we do not speak out when called to, we will be held accountable by God. Therefore we must speak out, regardless of whether the audience listens or responds appropriately (Ezekiel 3:11, 18-19; Ezekiel 33:1-9).

It is not enough to hear a prophecy and know that it is from God.

The Lord expects us to act upon it, responding appropriately to His words (Ezekiel 33:30-33). It is a mistake to suppose that any prophecy is for some time far off in the distant future; God may choose to fulfill it immediately (Ezekiel 12:25-28). Jeremiah 29:18-19 tells us that God allows the consequences to fall in full measure on those who ignore His warnings and reject opportunities for repentance.

A prophet's effectiveness is limited to those who recognize him or her as God's messenger. Familiarity, as the adage states and as Luke 4:24-27 indicates, breeds contempt, so people who know a prophet well are much more inclined to discount his messages as being from God.

Jonah discovered (Jonah 1:1-17) that when God wants something done, He'll find a way to accomplish it, which is usually more painful for the disobedient prophet than for a compassionate and cooperative one.

False prophets may be difficult to recognize (Matthew 7:15). They copy true prophets but they do not have the Holy Spirit within them to regulate them. As illustrated in Acts 16:16, fortune-telling is a form of counterfeit prophecy, which the Lord hates. All the prophets of God testify about Jesus and the forgiveness of sins through His name (Acts 2:30-31; Acts 10:43). Watch for the evidence of Spiritual fruit to validate the Holy Spirit's life within the prophet. (Keep in mind that Old Testament prophets did not always exhibit abundant Spiritual fruit because they did not have the indwelling Spirit. They had to rely on God's temporarily empowering them for specific circumstances.)

The attitude of love is the most important element in using any gift, as we are reminded in 1 Corinthians 13:2. It is particularly important in relation to prophecy, which can be frightening and discouraging if it is not accompanied by encouragement and hope. Eternity is unlimited by time measured as we know it. No prophecy will be needed when the future and the past are as current as the present. Understanding will be so much more complete in heaven that mere knowledge will be meaningless; and in the communion of our spirits, language of voices will be unnecessary. But love will be pervasive, unlimited, unhindered, uniting all in heaven as one, just as the Trinity—Father, Son, and Holy Spirit—is One.

As 1 Corinthians 14:1-5 and 22-26 tells us, the purpose of prophecy is to edify and strengthen the Church. It is intended for believers. Tongues edify ourselves and are a sign for unbelievers. (This is why, for purposes of edification, interpretation of tongues is so important). The four gifts of prophecy, edification, tongues, and interpretation may overlap, but all these gifts are needed for different purposes.

Order and courtesy enhance the prophetic message, as suggested in 1 Corinthians 14:29-31, 39-40; disorder detracts from it.

1 Thessalonians 5:19-21 commands us to not discourage people sent to minister to us, but to show respect for them and for their gifts. Yet we must test them to verify that they are truly from God, and hold fast to whatever is Godly.

Above all, the essence of prophecy is to give a clear witness for Jesus (Revelation 19:10).

Chapter 10

TONGUES

---

*Definition: The special ability to speak, in
a language the speaker has never learned,
a message given by the Holy Spirit*

Scriptures cited in Chapter 10 – Tongues

As a quality of God
Genesis 11:1
Genesis 4-9
Daniel 5:1-12

As illustrated in the Old Testament
Exodus 33: 9-11
Exodus 33:18-23
Exodus 34:33-35

As exemplified in Jesus' ministry
Exodus 33: 9-11
Exodus 33:18-23
Exodus 34:33-35
Matthew 27:50-51
Mark 15:37-38
Luke 23: 44-46
Hebrews 10:19-22
2 Corinthians 3:13-18
Matthew 19:26
Isaiah 29:13-14

As illustrated in the New Testament
Mark 16:15-17
Acts 2:4-16
Acts 2:4-16
1 Corinthians 14:10-13
1 Corinthians 14:22, 26-28
1 Corinthians 14:39-40

Related teachings
Revelation 2:17, 29
Revelation 3:6, 13, 22
Revelation 5:9-13
Revelation 7:9-12

Chapter 10

Tongues

Definition: The special ability to speak, in a language the speaker has never learned, a message given by the Holy Spirit [2]

As a quality of God

God saw that unity of language, referred to in Genesis 11:1 and 4-9, provided the people with strength to achieve the "impossible." In order to reserve that ability for Himself alone, He confused the language of the people and scattered the people across the earth. Only when His people are united to His Spirit does He unite us with Himself through languages we have not been taught during our earthly life. Until He does, we can converse with God, and He with us, only in our known languages. But our communication is limited to the extent of our understanding. When we have the gift of tongues, God can speak through us beyond our level of understanding. We are not limited by our known vocabulary.

God Himself wrote the unknown language on the wall of the banquet room, as described in Daniel 5:1-12. It was indecipherable to the learned men and those who practiced magic. But God provided an interpreter in the person of Daniel, as he was enabled by the Holy Spirit.

And God speaks to the hearts and minds of all His people, of every nation and every tongue, in language they can understand. Similarly He hears and responds to their prayers and supplications, whatever language they may use.

---

[2] The gift of tongues differs from prayer language (or praying in tongues) in that prayer language allows the Holy Spirit to intercede for the individual's own spirit to pray as the intellect cannot; the gift of tongues, however, is for the Church body—for prophecy, exhortation, and edification—and as a sign for non-believers.

As illustrated in the Old Testament

The Lord chose to whom He would speak directly. According to Exodus 33: 9-11, He spoke to Moses "as a man speaks with his friend." But the other people had to wait to hear God's word from Moses. In the same way, God speaks to one person, through the gifts of tongues and interpretation, to enlighten believers and unbelievers alike.

Just as Moses could not bear full exposure to God's face (Exodus 33:18-23), we cannot bear full exposure to His glory and omniscience. He protects us through language barriers from understanding too fully, just as He put Moses "in a cleft in the rock" and covered him until He had passed by.

The veil Moses used in Exodus 34:33-35 is also representative of a barrier of understanding. The people had not experienced what Moses had in the Lord's presence. They could share Moses' relationship with the Lord no more fully than Moses could comprehend the full extent of the Lord's glory. Yet when Moses spoke directly with the Lord, the veil was removed. In the same way, use of Spiritual tongues removes the language barriers between the Holy Spirit and the human spirit. Full understanding is kept from the human mind, but the spirit is given full access to God's presence.

As exemplified in Jesus' ministry

Like the veil Moses wore, the curtain in the Temple represented mankind's separation from the Most Holy Place (the Holy of Holies in the Temple), which represented the presence of God. When the curtain tore from top to bottom (Matthew 27:50-51; Mark 15:37-38; and Luke 23: 44-46) as Jesus died, the barrier was opened.

Believers suddenly were given direct access to God through Christ's sacrificial death. As Hebrews 10:19-22 puts it, we are given confidence to enter the Most Holy Place by the blood of Jesus. As believers in Christ, we can now communicate directly with God, both in prayer as our minds direct, and in tongues as the Holy Spirit enables us. But for unbelievers, the veil remains (2 Corinthians 3:13-18).

Human understanding and intellect actually oppose our relationship with God because human pride causes us to discount anything that is beyond our comprehension. If it is humanly inexplicable, then mankind is inclined to consider it impossible. Mankind tends to disbelieve that "with God all things are possible" (Matthew 19:26). But how could we worship a God whose omnipotence we discredit? Therefore, God circumvents our intellects by employing language we cannot comprehend (Isaiah 29:13-14). Our spirits know what our minds do not; so our spirits can worship as our minds cannot.

As illustrated in the New Testament

According to Mark 16:15-17, use of tongues is one of the signs that help identify believers.

The use of unknown tongues is also a sign to unbelievers (Acts 2:4-16), to confirm the validity of the believers' baptism in the Holy Spirit. Notice that the believers referred to in Acts 2:4-16 spoke "as the Spirit enabled them." They did not have to learn these new languages; they didn't have to know when or to whom to speak, but only to follow the enabling and direction of the Spirit of God. Notice also that it was the foreigners, the God-fearing Jews who did not yet know Christ, who recognized the sign and wanted to know the meaning of it. The witnessing was not consciously done by the believers, but they allowed the Holy Spirit to witness through them by the use of tongues.

1 Corinthians 14:10-13 tells us that all tongues have meaning. Although it can be a sign for unbelievers by itself, tongues do not edify the Church without interpretation. But the interpretation is available if we ask for it.

Remember the purpose. 1 Corinthians 14:22, 26-28 reminds us not to make a show of it or use it to call attention to ourselves. There is no point in speaking tongues aloud in public unless they can be interpreted. If there is no interpreter, the tongues are probably a personal prayer language to be reserved for private use between ourselves and God.

These are valuable gifts, as we are reminded in 1 Corinthians 14:39-40, though they appear odd to the world. They have a purpose and a place, but we need to remember that purpose, and use them at appropriate times and in appropriate ways, either in private prayer, or in public only when the Spirit directs or compels us, with faith for an interpretation.

Related teachings

When God repeats a message, as He does in Revelation 2:17; Revelation 2:29; Revelation 3:6; Revelation 3:13; and Revelation 3:22, its relative importance in magnified. It is clear that God wants the Church to listen to—and act upon—the messages the Spirit has for us.

The Revelation of John tells us that the multitude before God's throne were united in heart, in spirit, and in purpose. And despite language differences on earth, all were understood in heaven (Revelation 5:9-13; Revelation 7:9-12).

Chapter 11

INTERPRETATION

Definition: The special ability to express, in terms understood by the hearers, an interpretation or explanation, as provided by the Holy Spirit, including but not limited to prophecy or a manifestation of unknown tongues

---

Scriptures cited in Chapter 11 – Interpretation

As a quality of God
Job 42:1-6

As illustrated in the Old Testament
Genesis 41:15-37
Daniel 5:13-17
Daniel 5:18-24
Daniel 5:25-31

As exemplified in Jesus' ministry
John 11:41-42
Matthew 13:18-52
Matthew 15:15-20
Luke 24:27
John 12:46-50
John 14:7-10
Matthew 5:17-26
Matthew 5:43-48
Matthew 6:1

As illustrated in the New Testament
Acts 8:30-35
1 Corinthians 12:7-11

Related teachings
1 Corinthians 14:2-19
1 Corinthians 14:26-28

Chapter 11
Interpretation

> *Definition: The special ability to express, in terms understood by the hearers, an interpretation or explanation, as provided by the Holy Spirit, including but not limited to prophecy or a manifestation of unknown tongues*

As a quality of God

Whatever language we use to communicate with God, He understands and replies in kind so we can understand His response.

When, like Job (Job 42:1-6), we do not understand something, we can ask the Lord for the answers. His purposes are often obscured by false assumptions that come from our limited human understanding. If we seek His mind, He will clarify—interpret—for us whatever He wants us to understand.

As illustrated in the Old Testament

Genesis 41:15-37 tells us: "Pharaoh said to Joseph, 'I had a dream, but no one can interpret it. But I have heard it said of you that when you hear a dream you can interpret it.'" Joseph proceeded to listen to Pharaoh's account of his dreams and provided the explanation of them so Pharaoh could take appropriate steps to prepare for the coming famine.

King Balshazzar also attempted unsuccessfully to obtain interpretations, from both human advisors and from his false gods, of the writing he had watched appear on the wall (Daniel 5:13-17). Daniel rejected the promise of payment and benefits offered to him for what God was doing through him. He did not want to accept rewards but fulfilled the king's request simply because He knew that the message was from God and that God had appointed him to provide the interpretation.

Daniel reviewed the mistakes of the king's father (Daniel 5:18-24), reminding the king that Balshazzar's father had fallen because of pride, and pointing out that Belshazzar had not learned from his father's mistakes. He revealed that this message, written in an unknown tongue, was a decree from God.

Daniel gave the interpretation boldly, bluntly, and without apology or uncertainty (Daniel 5:25-31). Only the God of Daniel could reveal the interpretation of this foreign tongue, which, in this case, had been written directly by God's emissary hand. The message was verified that same night by its fulfillment. Daniel was honored, not because he had sought the honor but because he had proven true to God's calling.

As exemplified in Jesus' ministry

Scripture does not tell us that Jesus interpreted tongues, but He did interpret and explain His relationship with the Father so that others could benefit from that understanding (John 11:41-42). And He interpreted for His disciples the meaning of His parables (Matthew 13:18-52; Matthew 15:15-20). After His resurrection, He also revealed to them the references in scripture, concerning Himself, through Moses and the prophets (Luke 24:27).

In John 12:46-50, Jesus also explained—interpreted—His purpose, revealing His own dependence upon the Father. By His example, we know that, just as Jesus spoke only what the Father commanded, one who interprets tongues or prophecy must speak only what the Holy Spirit commands.

Jesus Himself was the interpretation of God (John 14:7-10): "Anyone who has seen Me," He said, "has seen the Father."

Moses had made known to the people the law of God. But it became distorted through worldly misinterpretations. Jesus' teachings in Matthew 5:17-26 served to interpret and clarify both the extent and the intent of law. In Matthew 5:43-48, to bring us toward God's own perfect standard of holiness, Jesus simplified and clarified the Mosaic law, which had been lost in hypocrisy. Jesus reinterpreted the law according to God's original intent, reminding His listeners that they were to seek God's approval, not the approval or notice of men (Matthew 6:1).

As illustrated in the New Testament

Acts 8:30-35 clearly shows the Holy Spirit's deliberately placing Philip in the path of the Ethiopian in order to meet his spiritual needs by interpreting or explaining scripture for him.

Interpretation of tongues is referred to specifically in 1 Corinthians 12:7-11 as a gift and as being necessary and valuable to use in conjunction with the gift of tongues because, without an interpretation, the edifying value of messages given in tongues is lost to the body of the Church, which it is intended to edify.

Related teachings

The Apostle Paul explains, in 1 Corinthians 14:2-19, that tongues, which are spoken (as provided by the Holy Spirit) to God, must also be interpreted by the Holy Spirit in order for the Church to understand and benefit from the message.

This theme is reiterated in 1 Corinthians 14:26-28: Messages from God are important to the Church body, but someone must interpret them by the power of the Holy Spirit in order for the Church to benefit.

Chapter 12

EDIFICATION

Definition: The special ability to build up the Church body spiritually through encouragement and greater appreciation of God

---

Scriptures cited in Chapter 12 – Edification

As a quality of God
Exodus 5:22-23
Exodus 6:1-13
Exodus chs 7-12
Judges 6:11-24
1 King 19:3-18
Daniel 10:10-19
Isaiah 57:14-19
Acts 18:9-10
Acts 23:11

As illustrated in the Old Testament
1 Samuel 23:15-16
1 Chronicles 12:18
2 Chronicles 20:14-20
Daniel 10:16-19
Jeremiah 42:9-12
Haggai 2:1-9

As exemplified in Jesus' ministry
Mark 6:45-51
Acts 1:3

As illustrated in the New Testament
Luke 10:9
Acts 11:22-24
Acts 13:15
Acts 13:43-44
Acts 13:47-49
Acts 15:22-32
Acts 15:36-41
Acts 16:40
1 Thessalonians 3:2-3
Acts 20:32
Acts 18:27

Related teachings
Nehemiah 4:6-23
Ephesians 4:29
Proverbs 12:18,:25
Proverbs 14:1
Proverbs 15:4, 28, 30
Acts 12:17
Philippians 4:8
Hebrews 3:13

Chapter 12
Edification

> *Definition: The special ability to build up the Church body spiritually through encouragement and greater appreciation of God*

As a quality of God

When Moses was discouraged by the plight of the Israelites in Egypt, God offered him hope by reminding him of His authority and covenants with previous generations and by pointing out that even the Patriarchs were not on a first-name basis with God as Moses was (Exodus 5:22-23; Exodus 6:1-13). When the Israelites did not listen to him because of their fears of Pharaoh's retribution, Moses remained uncertain. But God commanded Moses and Aaron to do as He said, and "multiplied signs and wonders in Egypt" (Exodus chs. 7-12) to convince Pharaoh to forcibly drive them out. Only by exercising obedience to God would the Israelites recognize God's supreme power to overcome Pharaoh's lesser authority, and would they learn to trust in God's deliverance and leadership through Moses. God was able to edify and thereby encourage them even through the seemingly unbearable burdens they were experiencing.

When the angel of the Lord charged Gideon with saving Israel from Midian, Gideon asked how he could possibly save Israel, his clan being the weakest in the area, and he being the least of his family (Judges 6:11-24). The Lord encouraged him (v. 16) and assured him of victory. Even then, Gideon asked for further reassurance. And God provided it. When Gideon realized that he had "seen the angel of the LORD face to face" he must have been terrified, "But the LORD said to him, 'Peace! Do not be afraid. You are not going to die'" (v. 23).

When the prophet Elijah was running for his life (1 King 19:3-18) and was ready to give up, he too encountered an angel of the Lord who provided physical nourishment and spiritual assurance.

Likewise, Daniel was directly encouraged, though God's messenger was delayed by spiritual warfare with Satan, the "prince of the Persian kingdom" (Daniel 10:10-19). Ultimately Daniel said, "May my lord speak, for you have strengthened me."

Notice in Isaiah 57:14-19 whom God blesses with His presence, and why. God knows that without encouragement and a greater understanding and appreciation of Him, we would become too discouraged by our failures to continue. God is holy and recognizes our sinful and willful ways, but in His love and mercy, He chooses to heal and encourage us anyway, lightening the hearts of those who mourn over their sins, who are repentant and contrite.

In the New Testament, the Lord renewed the Apostle Paul's sense of purpose through edification whenever he might have begun questioning his purpose and safety (Acts 18:9-10; Acts 23:11).

As illustrated in the Old Testament

Whether Jonathan was responding to a prompting by the Holy Spirit at Horesh (1 Sam 23:15-16), we don't know, but his encouragement "helped [David] find strength in God." However, we are clearly told that the Spirit moved Amasai (1 Chronicles 12:18) to similarly edify and encourage David.

The Spirit of the LORD also came upon Jahaziel specifically to offer edification and encouragement to King Jehoshaphat and the Judeans, as recorded in 2 Chronicles 20:14-20.

Edification could come directly from the Holy Spirit, from "an angel of the Lord" (like that in Daniel 10:16-19) or through prophecy (as recorded in Jeremiah 42:9-12 and in Haggai 2:1-9).

As exemplified in Jesus' ministry

As we read Mark 6:45-51, in which Jesus sent His disciples in a boat across the Sea of Galilee, and later walked across the water to them, we can only speculate about why Jesus "was about to pass by them" (v. 48). Perhaps He was just checking on their peace of mind but intended to cross ahead of them to be waiting for them in Bethsaida. In any case, as soon as the disciples became frightened upon seeing Him, He reassured them verbally and then climbed into the boat to reassure them with His physical presence as well. The wind died down also, showing that, in His mercy, He also eased the burden of the struggles they had been facing. "They were completely amazed" because they hadn't recognized, before that, the extent of His power. Little by little He was edifying them—building them up—into the strong Church He wanted them to become.

What could have been more encouraging and edifying regarding Jesus' resurrection than His repeated appearance in the flesh, to numerous believers, as recorded in Acts 1:3? Through this remarkable assurance—incontrovertible evidence of the continuation of life after death—we are edified about the nature of God Himself, the sacrificial love of the Lord, and are encouraged by His continuing presence with us through the power of the indwelling Spirit of the Living God.

As illustrated in the New Testament

Edification can come in many forms, one of which is the evidence of physical healing, which offers assurance that God is merciful and that spiritual healing is available from Him as well (Luke 10:9).

Encouragement goes in two directions, as it did in Acts 11:22-24, in which Barnabas was gladdened by seeing evidence of the grace of God, while encouraging and strengthening the church in Antioch.

Any encouragement and edification available to the Church should be given (Acts 13:15). People may become overwhelmed by their failures and tend to lose hope when they realize that the ancient prophecies were directed to people such as themselves who were unable to conform fully to the Law. They, like sinners today, needed to hear a message of encouragement and hope of sanctification by the forgiveness of sins through the blood of Christ.

We see in Acts 13:43-44 and Acts 13:47-49, that encouragement is attractive. It attracts everyone, Jews and Gentiles alike, who hunger for hope and purpose.

As exemplified in Acts 15:22-32, encouragement involves expressing empathy over concerns, lightening burdens rather than adding to them, and renewing a sense of hope and purpose.

Barnabas' name meant "son of encouragement," and in fact, he did seem to be a great encourager in the early Church. As related in Acts 15:36-41, it appears that John Mark had abandoned the Apostle Paul on their first mission trip. Paul was anxious to continue the work but wasn't willing to take a risk with John Mark again. He knew that both his life and the work could be jeopardized by a deserter, so instead he took Silas, whom he felt he could trust. Barnabas, however, apparently was as concerned about John Mark's future as he was with the mission. He knew that John Mark could give up on his work or even fail in his Christian walk if he weren't encouraged to return to his original calling. So when Paul refused to take a chance with him, Barnabas took John Mark under his own wing and set out on a separate mission to continue the work and to encourage John Mark. In this way, not only was John Mark strengthened, but the mission work branched out as well.

It should be noted in this passage that although Paul did not feel led to edify John Mark, he still successfully responded to the call to edify the churches, "strengthening" them. We mustn't be critical of someone for responding—or not responding—to the apparent call of a gift in any specific way. His call may be in a different direction or have a different focus from someone else's, using the same Spiritual gift, and still be just as necessary and just as effective. It's not for us to judge. Only God knows for what purpose each of us is called.

The encouragement of personal testimony of God's victory over earthly situations, as Paul and Silas provided when they came out of prison (Acts 16:40), helps believers refocus on God rather than on their present difficulties.

Even when we know we're facing tribulation, edification in understanding God and being reminded of His continuing presence helps us prepare for our trials and encourages us through them (1 Thessalonians 3:2-3).

Acts 20:32 tells us that the gospel—the good news of God's grace—is the greatest encouragement anyone can share.

We also see in Acts 18:27 that encouragement supports other Spiritual gifts.

Related teachings

In Nehemiah 4:6-23, we find a strong parallel with the situation today's Church faces. The "people" referred to in the scriptural passage may be likened to today's Christians who are doing their best to live a faithful, service-filled life. "Foreigners" (vv. 7-8), representative of satanic forces, continue to plot against the purposes of the Church.

Christians are to pray to support the Godly forces in such spiritual warfare and keep alert to encroaching trouble. When we see the amount of work still to be done, we may begin to think that all our hard work is pointless and forget to look at what has already been accomplished; it's easy to become discouraged. Satan continues to plot, intending to sneak in when we are unaware, with the intention of destroying us and stopping the work of God. The world, too, sends us discouraging messages (v. 12). Some of these are from non-Christians, others from carnal Christians—notice that they live nearby and are expecting the benefits of the work without participating in the work themselves.

The "family groups" (v. 13) represent local churches, each one on the alert for its own members, but working in unison to protect the work of the Church as a whole. We need to remember the power of the Lord and that we are protecting our own home interests as well as providing for the overall goal, laboring by day and on the alert by night.

We are encouraged by good reports of God's victories, so that we can continue in our work for Him. There is power in good reports. As we continue to recognize parallels throughout this passage from Nehemiah, we can identify some of us as laborers, others as watchmen and intercessors. The leaders should make themselves available to guide and encourage the workers. Everyone must remain alert and ready to defend the work of the Church. And God is still the rallying point for everyone in case of an attack. The local churches are spread out across the entire earth, often separated by great distances, both geographically and culturally, from one another. But when God calls us, we close ranks spiritually, rallying to His cause, and God fights side by side with us. In this way we must continue the work that God has given us to do, always on the alert against Satan's schemes, twenty-four hours a day, seven days a week, never letting down our guard for a moment (vv. 22-23).

Ephesians 4:29 reminds us to "not let any unwholesome talk come out of your mouths, but only what is helpful for building others up according to their needs, that it may benefit those who listen."

King Solomon also offered applicable pearls of wisdom throughout Proverbs. Take special note of Proverbs 12:18; 12:25; 14:1; 15:4; 15:28; and 15:30.

We are to receive and share encouraging news with others, especially in times of fear or trouble, as Peter did in Acts 12:17.

Philippians 4:8 exhorts us to keep our own minds on positive thoughts: "whatever is true, whatever is noble, whatever is right, whatever is pure, whatever is lovely, whatever is admirable—if anything is excellent or praiseworthy—think about such things."

And Hebrews 3:13 reminds us to "encourage one another daily, as long as it is called Today, so that none of you may be hardened by sin's deceitfulness."

Chapter 13

EXHORTATION

Definition: The special ability to effectively call others to repentance or to a higher level of spiritual growth through rebuking, correcting, admonishing, and giving warnings or advice

---

Scriptures cited in Chapter 13 -- Exhortation

As a quality of God
Exodus 34:10-27
Leviticus 10:1-3
1 Kings 6:11-13
1 Kings 9:1-3
1 Kings 9:4-5
1 Kings 9:6-9
Job 33:14-30
Psalm 19:9-11
Psalm 23:4
Psalm 78:34-35
Nahum 1:2-7
Acts 3:26

As illustrated in the Old Testament
Deuteronomy 11:1-8
1 Samuel 12:6-25
1 Samuel 15:10-24
2 Samuel 12:1-13
1 Chronicles 22:11-13
2 Chronicles 29:3-15
2 Chronicles 30:6-13
Ezra 10:10-14
Nehemiah 5:9-12
Nehemiah 13:6-13
Nehemiah 13:23-28
Haggai 1:2-12

As exemplified in Jesus' ministry
Matthew 26:41
Mark 8:33
Luke 7:39-50
John 8:26
Matthew. 21:12-13
John 2:15

As illustrated in the New Testament
Acts 2:14-41
1 Corinthians 3:10-15
Galatians 1:6-12
Galatians 6:1
Ephesians 4:1-3
Ephesians 5:1-2
Philippians. 2:3-6
Philippians 3:2
Galatians 2:11
1Timothy 2:1-4

Related teachings
2 Corinthians 10:3-5
Ephesians 5:11-18
Esther 4:14
Ezekiel 3:20-21
Job 42:7-9
Job 33:6-7
1 Timothy1:3-5
1 Timothy 5:19-20
Hebrews 12:5-11
1 Timothy 5:1-2
2 Corinthians 13:10
Galatians 6:1-2
Proverbs 13:24
Proverbs 29:15
Psalm 38:2-5
Judges 2:15-22
1 Samuel 3:11-13
2 Kings 17:12-20
Job 36:8-12
Proverbs 1:23-33
Proverbs 10:17
Psalm 94:12

Psalm 119:9-16, 23-24, 36-37, 67
Psalm 141:5
Acts 3:19
2 Corinthians 13:11
1 Thessalonians 5:12-13

Chapter 13
Exhortation

> *Definition: The special ability to effectively call others to repentance or to a higher level of spiritual growth through rebuking, correcting, admonishing, and giving warnings or advice*

As a quality of God

God, in Exodus 34:10-27, exhorted His people in order to protect them from their own foolishness and from outside influences. He admonished, warned, and gave specific directions to ensure their well-being, assuring them of His protection from perceived earthly risks they would take by obeying Him. He also provided reminders, for both themselves and future generations, by having His instructions written down for later reference.

God used Aaron's sons as an example to warn the entire nation of the destruction that comes through sin (Leviticus 10:1-3). In recognizing God's righteousness in carrying out His judgment, Aaron held his tongue probably because of the conviction he felt for his own role in the inadequacy of their training.

God's admonition is also seen when he gave specific reminders to Solomon regarding construction and furnishing of the Temple (1 Kings 6:11-13), combined with a renewal of the promise He had previously made to King David. Later, when the Temple was completed, God began further exhortation by providing assurance of having heard Solomon's prayer and of His having consecrated the Temple (1 Kings 9:1-3). God renewed the promise He had made to David, again offering Solomon reassurance (1 Kings 9:4-5). But recognizing Solomon's human weaknesses, He also warned him of the severe and long-term consequences of subsequent faithlessness (1 Kings 9:6-9).

As Elihu reminded Job (Job 33:14-30), God exhorts each of us in different ways according to His knowledge of our needs. In every case the purpose is to protect us in this present life and save us from eternal condemnation. God's ultimate purpose is to show us His grace in the face of our faithlessness and thereby bring glory to Him (v.27).

Psalm 19:9-11 reminds us of the rightness, value, and benefit of God's ordinances and that we are greatly benefited by heeding the prodding of the One who cares so deeply for us. The rod, representing discipline, and the staff, representing guidance, both cited in Psalm 23:4, assure us of God's continuing concerned involvement in our lives.

Even when God has to resort to extreme methods (Psalm 78:34-35), His purpose in exhortation is always to draw His people into closer relationship with Him.

God's judgment is righteous and no one can withstand His vengeance. But He is also gracious, and He protects those who heed His warnings and directions, those who trust in Him for their salvation (Nahum 1:2-7).

God's desire is to bless us by leading us from sinfulness into a life of righteousness (Acts 3:26).

As illustrated in the Old Testament

Moses exhorted the Hebrews in Deuteronomy 11:1-8, reminding them of their past experiences under God's protection and admonishing them to remain faithful to His instructions to them. In this way their slackening commitment was reinforced and they were prepared to exercise their faith, taking it to the next level of spiritual growth.

Samuel, too, exhorted the people (1 Samuel 12:6-25), reminding them of God's faithfulness in having led the Hebrews out of Egypt and in providing the help they would need on the journey and in their new land (vv. 1-8). He reminded them of the consequences of disobedience (v.9) and of God's faithfulness in responding to true repentance (vv. 10-11). Samuel then rebuked the people for their rebellion (vv. 12-17). They were convicted and repented of their sin (vv. 18-19). He left them with both assurance of God's faithfulness to His people and a warning that there would be drastic consequences if they did not remain faithful to the Lord (vv. 20-25). He also recognized his own responsibility to pray for them, though whether he was praying in intercession or for wisdom in knowing how to counsel them is not indicated.

When King Saul turned away from the Lord, Samuel knew that the consequences of the king's disobedience would fall on the entire nation (1 Samuel 15:10-24). Samuel confronted Saul about his disobedience and his self-deception (vv. 12-23). The result was Saul's repentance (v. 24).

Similarly, Nathan had to exhort King David to bring about repentance. Nathan presented a hypothetical situation to illustrate the sin that needed to be brought to light (2 Samuel 12:1-13). It was easier for David to recognize someone else's sin than to acknowledge his own. But when Nathan revealed the identity of the sinner and the consequences of the sin, the exhortation resulted in David's repentance and in Nathan's assurance of God's forgiveness. The consequences of King David's sin, however, still had to be faced. Repentance did not alter the results of his sinful actions.

King David admonished Solomon, as recorded in 1 Chronicles 22:11-13, reminding him that discretion and understanding would come from the Lord and that success would depend on his obedience to the Lord's direction.

King Hezekiah reminded the Levites of their fathers' disobedience and the resulting consequences (2 Chronicles 29:3-15). He then called them to commit themselves to a higher level of faithfulness, caring for the Temple and ministering to the Lord, as their heritage ordained. Many of the Levites responded to the call. Hezekiah also exhorted the nation (2 Chronicles 30:6-13), admonishing, advising, and warning them through the message carried by his couriers. Although many people rejected the message, many others responded to the call to greater spiritual obedience. Godly exhortation will not always be completely successful, but it will succeed with those people who are responsive to the Lord's guidance and correction.

Ezra rebuked the people for their unfaithfulness (Ezra 10:10-14). He not only corrected them by identifying the specific area of failure, but he recommended what they should do about it. The people acknowledged their sin, repented, and took steps to correct the situation.

Nehemiah also exhorted the people, identifying a specific sin and advising the people about how to rectify it (Nehemiah 5:9-12). The people repented, and Nehemiah made the leaders take an oath that they would follow through on changing their ways. In Nehemiah 13:6-13, Nehemiah again identified a specific sin and saw that it was corrected. He rebuked the officials and took steps to rectify the wrongs that had been done. Exhortation includes not only warnings about avoiding sin but also guidance in correcting wrongs after they have been committed. The purpose of Nehemiah's rebukes in Nehemiah 13:23-28, as always, was to bring about repentance and correction.

Because our natural tendency is to focus our energies and interests more on ourselves than on the Lord, on our own concerns than on His, the basic message of Godly exhortation might perhaps best be stated with the Lord's words in Haggai 1:2-12, "Give careful thought to your ways." Godly exhortation instills a healthy respect for the Lord and serves to redirect our will to align with His.

As exemplified in Jesus' ministry

Jesus understood firsthand the weakness of the flesh, so He not only admonished His followers regarding what they should do but explained the reasoning behind why they should do it (Matthew 26:41).

In Mark 8:33, Jesus, who experienced for Himself the continual struggle between the spirit and the flesh, exposed both the tempter and the conflict as a warning to His disciples about the source of their weakness and as a reminder of where their concerns should be.

In His own exhortations, such as that in Luke 7:39-50, Jesus maintained an attitude of loving compassion. Jesus opened His comments to Simon in such a tone as to leave Simon open to hear what He had to say. He did not rebuke him on the spot or put him on the defensive. Jesus posed His question kindly, in such a way that Simon could answer correctly. When he did, Jesus commended him for making the proper judgment. Again, He avoided putting Simon on the defensive. This left Simon's heart and mind open to learn (vv. 41-43).

Jesus drew a simple comparison, the truth of which was indisputable (vv. 44-46). Jesus clearly identified the principle He was teaching, and He used Simon's own answer to illustrate the point He wanted to make (v.47). Everything was said with gentleness, love, and consideration. When Jesus reassured the woman whose sins had been discussed, it was in such a way that any embarrassment that she might have felt over the discussion was diffused (v.48). When His authority was challenged, opening the possibility of doubt being raised in the woman's mind, Jesus reassured her once again with the explanation and a blessing (vv. 49, 50). Again, everything was said in gentleness and love, nothing in anger or indignation. The woman was forgiven and blessed, Simon was corrected and given the opportunity to grow spiritually, and the other guests had witnessed Christ's love in action. In this single exhortation, Jesus successfully showed us how to restore a sinner without demeaning anyone involved.

As He pointed out in John 8:26, Jesus had both good reason and the right to be judgmental of us; His own righteousness far exceeded anyone else's. Yet He rebuked and corrected only as the Father directed Him to, demonstrating love, gentleness, and kindness to those who turned to Him.

On the other hand, when blatant disregard was shown for the holiness of the Temple, Jesus reacted in righteous indignation for the contempt expressed for His Father's house (Matthew 21:12-13; John 2:15). This was not to elicit repentance from the guilty parties but to cleanse the Temple of its defilement.

As illustrated in the New Testament

As we can see in Acts 2:14-41, on the day of Pentecost, the Apostle Peter addressed the gathered crowd in Jerusalem, reminding them of the prophetic promises that foretold that day's events. He exhorted them to repent and believe. His effective exhortation resulted in repentance and spiritual growth for many of his listeners (v. 41).

Paul wrote to the Corinthians (1 Corinthians 3:10-15), exhorting them in his letters to build carefully on the foundation of Christ, which Paul had already provided through his teachings, admonishing them that the quality of each person's work would become evident through testing at the final judgment.

Paul's letter to the Galatians (Galatians 1:6-12) exhorted that church to reject false gospels that distorted the truth he had already taught them, which had been received directly by a revelation of Jesus Christ—a gospel not of works but of grace. In closing (Galatians 6:1), he directed them to correct one another in a spirit of gentleness and humility, much as he had just demonstrated in his own exhortations to them.

He exhorted the Ephesians, also, to live in a manner worthy of their calling, in gentleness, humility, and patience (Ephesians 4:1-3), being imitators of God (Ephesians 5:1-2). The recurring exhortation to live humbly in Christ's likeness (Philippians 2:3-6) challenged believers to seek a higher spiritual level, while repeated warnings regarding false teachings (Philippians 3:2) were made as protection for the believers' spiritual wellbeing. Both themes appear frequently throughout the New Testament epistles.

When Paul called Peter's attention to Peter's hypocrisy to give him the opportunity to correct his ways (Galatians 2:11), Paul's purpose was not to demean Peter but to correct a problem and to help him grow spiritually. Paul pointed out in 1 Timothy 2:1-4 that God's purpose in all exhortation—even in how to pray for others—is that all people should be saved and should increase in their understanding of Him.

Related teachings

We cannot fight God's battles effectively by earthly means (2 Corinthians 10:3-5). The world fights with anger and hate and violence. God's weapons, on the other hand, include love, joy, Spiritual peace, patience, kindness, goodness, gentleness, and self-control—the very nature of God Himself. He has also provided us with "the full armor of God" (Ephesians 5:11-18) for protection and defense in the war that is continuously being waged against us.

When God places us in a position to speak out, we should be obedient to His leading. Godly exhortation benefits the entire body of God's people, for it promotes restoration, healing, and unity. Queen Esther had risen to the position of most-favored wife of a king who was being manipulated to destroy God's people. Her uncle exhorted her by pointing out that that situation could have been the very purpose for which God had prepared her and placed her into such an influential position (Esther 4:14).

We will be held accountable by God for the exhorting He gives us to do (Ezekiel 3:20-21). He takes it seriously, and so should we. As we are shown in Job 42:7-9, if we are to rebuke others, we must be sure that our rebuke is well founded and that our understanding of God's will is accurate. As Godly exhorters, we should be humble, avoid condescension, and remember that we ourselves are fallible and are also under God's sovereignty (Job 33:6-7).

One of our callings as faithful, Spirit-filled Christians is to be watchful that teaching is true to Scripture and that the Church remains true to its calling (1Timothy1:3-5). Any sin, but especially that of a person in public ministry, denigrates the public perception of Godliness. Therefore, sins that have come to light are to be rebuked publicly so that the true perception of God's holiness is restored. But because people in leadership roles are particularly subject to false accusations, any charges need to be verified before a public rebuke is made (1 Timothy 5:19-20). The purpose of Godly exhortation is always to restore and promote the development of God-like character (Hebrews 12:5-11), never to demean or bring public shame.

Rebukes are to be made in a spirit of restorative love, with respect and gentleness (1Timothy 5:1-2). God's purpose is to build the body, not to destroy it; to build our faith, not to undermine it (2 Corinthians 13:10).

Gentleness is important in restoring a sinner (Galatians 6:1-2). As exhorters, we must be careful not to become prideful or overly self-confident because Satan can use that to cause our own downfall. We need one another. It is much easier to see other people's shortcomings than to acknowledge our own, so exhorters should be ready to accept exhortation from others as well.

Correction can come in many forms. If we love, we must provide care-filled (not spite-filled) discipline, even when it is painful (Proverbs 13:24). The difference between discipline and punishment lies in the purpose and the exercise of self-control. Loving, constructive discipline provides an opportunity for learning and growth so that, long-term, the person develops self-control (Proverbs 29:15). Punishment, on the other hand, is usually reactive without necessarily promoting the development of self-control. An accurate and well presented rebuke, directed by God, brings conviction and repentance (Psalm 38:2-5).

Godly exhortation is for God's purposes, and there are serious consequences when it is ignored. The Lord allowed Israel to feel consequences of their disobedience, about which they had been warned (Judges 2:15-22). Although He showed them mercy by providing judges to exhort them to follow and obey Him, Israel continued to turn away in increasing disobedience. In order to restore them through repentance, God finally allowed them to experience the suffering from which He had tried to protect them.

In 1 Samuel 3:11-13, God had already warned Eli about his sons' sin, but Eli had failed to exhort them effectively. Therefore, the Lord spoke to Samuel, who was also being raised by Eli, to clarify God's purpose of His coming judgment on the family. It was to serve as a rebuke to Eli specifically, as a warning to Israel generally, and as admonishment for Samuel's faithful obedience.

Israel and Judah discovered, in 2 Kings 17:12-20, that disregard of God's warnings and corrections led to painful consequences. God does not abandon His desire to draw us into closer relationship with Himself; but when we rebel against Him, He must resort to harsher, more painful means of establishing His authority. As we see in Job 36:8-12, sometimes He must leave us to our own devices until we realize that, without His help, we will perish. Everyone has a choice to repent or continue in sin. The decision will have its own consequences.

Ignoring correction leads to destruction (Proverbs 1:23-33) not only of self but of others (Proverbs 10:17). But we benefit and are blessed if we take God's exhortation to heart (Psalm 94:12). Discipline is developed by attention and obedience to God's word (Psalm 119:9-16, 23-24, 36-37, 67). It also comes from corrections from Godly friends (Psalm 141:5). Our response to exhortation should be repentance from sin (Acts 3:19) with an aim toward Godly perfection (2 Corinthians 13:11). And we should respect and honor those whom God has used to bring about our spiritual growth and protection (1 Thessalonians 5:12-13). Whereas human modes of discipline may be faulty, unwisely administered or from selfish motivations, God only disciplines us to promote the development of a more God-like character within us.

Chapter 14

KNOWLEDGE

Definition: The special ability to sense information that cannot be learned in the natural but only through revelation from God

---

Scriptures cited in Chapter 14 – Knowledge

As a quality of God
Exodus 3:7-22
Exodus 16:4-5
Job 36:3-4
Psalm 139:1-16
Isaiah. 55:8-9
1 Corinthians 2:11-13

As illustrated in the Old Testament
Deuteronomy 31:29
Habakkuk 2:2-4
Daniel 1:17-20
Daniel 2:16-19
Judges 7:13-15
Judges 13:2-23
1 Samuel 9:15-17
1 Samuel 16:6-13
1 Samuel 23:9-13
1 Samuel 30:7-8
2 Samuel 5:18-19
1 Samuel 28:5-10
1 Kings 14:1-18
1 Kings 17:1-9
2 Kings 2:1-6
2 Kings 6:15-17
2 Kings 6:31-32
2 Kings 8:8-15
1 Chronicles 14:13-16
Daniel. 1:17-20
Daniel 2:10-11
Daniel 2:46-47
Habakkuk 1:5

As exemplified in Jesus' ministry
Luke 2:46-47
Matthew 12:25-37
Mark 2:8

John 6:64
Matthew 17:24-27
Mark 5:39
John 7:14-16

As illustrated in the New Testament
Luke 1:41-45
Acts 1:26
Acts 7:55-56
Acts 8:26-29
Acts 9:10-16
Acts 10:1-6
Acts 10:19-20
Acts 27:23-26
2 Corinthians 12:1-6
Ephesians 1:9-10
Ephesians 3:2-6
2 Peter 1:13-15

Related teachings
Habakkuk 2:14
Psalm 25:14
Jeremiah. 33:3
Psalm 16:7
John 6:45
Psalm 43:3
Psalm 49:3
Psalm 73:15-17
Psalm 119:34
Psalm 119:66, 169
Proverbs 1:7
Proverbs 1:23
Proverbs 15:14
Proverbs 20:15
Leviticus 19:31
Proverbs 14:7;

Romans 1:21-32
1 Timothy 6:20-21
Proverbs 2:1-6).
Proverbs 3:31-32
Acts 1:7
Proverbs 12:23
Proverbs 19:2
Proverbs 17:27
Proverbs 13:16
Proverbs 30:5-6
1 Timothy 6:20-21

Knowledge

> *Definition: The special ability to sense information that cannot be learned in the natural but only through revelation from God*

As a quality of God

God is omniscient—all-knowing—of the past, the present, and the future. He is knowledgeable about our every situation. Exodus 3:7-22 illustrates for us that He knows what we have experienced and what still lies ahead of us. He also knows what our adversaries will do and is both willing and able to counsel us in how to proceed.

God took the initiative to assure Moses during the flight from Egypt by giving him knowledge of how the need for food would be met, what to do with it, and His purpose for providing in this manner (Exodus 16:4-5). Without God's revelation, Moses would not have been able to instruct the people knowledgeably or encourage them that their food would be provided on a daily basis.

God's knowledge is both perfect and just (Job 36:3-4). His knowledge of us is intimate and ever-present, far surpassing the capabilities of human knowledge (Psalm 139:1-16; Isaiah 55:8-9).

1 Corinthians 2:11-13 tells us that "no one knows the thoughts of God except the Spirit of God." We have access to His thoughts only as He imparts them through His Holy Spirit to us.

As illustrated in the Old Testament

Knowledge and prophecy often overlap. Where prophecy often provides warning of impending trouble, knowledge explains the cause, provocation, or reason for the delay before fulfillment (Deuteronomy 31:29; Habakkuk 2:2-4). Spiritual knowledge can be provided through a vision or dream (Daniel 1:17-20; Daniel 2:16-19). In Judges 7:13-15 knowledge was combined with the interpretation for a clearer revelation.

Knowledge could be revealed by an angel or through another spokesperson (prophecy) in response to a direct request for knowledge (Judges 13:2-23). The request for pertinent information was often honored, while unneeded information or inappropriate knowledge was withheld (v. 18).

God used a word of knowledge to call or commission someone for a particular task and to guide its progress, as we see in 1 Samuel 9:15-17. Samuel began a search (1 Samuel 16:6-13), based on his human intellect, for the man God had called him to anoint as king. But God corrected Samuel's thinking and reminded him to trust the Lord's knowledge rather than his own. As he listened for the Lord's confirmation of each man, Samuel was not satisfied that he had seen all the possibilities. At the right time and in the right circumstances, the Lord revealed the knowledge of His choice of king. Samuel was obedient in completing the mission God had given him, then went on about his other work, trusting that the Lord would lead David from that point on, just as he himself had been led.

When David needed guidance from the Lord (1 Samuel 23:9-13; 1 Samuel 30:7-8; 2 Samuel 5:18-19), he requested that the ephod, the priest's garment, be brought because it contained the Urim and Thummim, items traditionally used to reveal God's responses to direct questions. In this way David was able to seek and obtain knowledge that only God could provide. David repeatedly consulted God in faith, and the Lord answered. When Saul sought knowledge out of fear rather than in faith, however, God remained silent (1 Samuel 28:5-10). Saul then foolishly turned to the occult, against his own orders and against the will of God, to obtain knowledge that God had already chosen not to reveal.

The knowledge God revealed to Ahijah in 1 Kings 14:1-18 allowed the prophet, despite his physical blindness, to immediately see through Jeroboam's wife's disguise. This knowledge enhanced and underscored the credibility of his prophecy.

God provides knowledge to protect His servants and to sustain them in times of severe difficulty as He did for Elijah (1 Kings 17:1-9).

In the face of Elisha's denial of the inevitable and his

self-determination to continue serving Elijah rather than humbly obeying Elijah's directions (2 Kings 2:1-6), God twice provided knowledge to confirm the impending separation so that Elisha could have no doubt that it was in the Lord's plan.

Knowledge can provide reassurance of God's understanding and control over seemingly insurmountable situations in our lives (2 Kings 6:15-17). It can provide warnings or reveal motives (2 Kings 6:31-32). God sometimes humors us by providing the false assurance that we demand, but always accompanied by more extensive and contradictory knowledge of the truth, revealed through discernment and prophecy (2 Kings 8:8-15).

God may reveal timing and strategy to be used to overcome an enemy (1 Chronicles 14:13-16). His knowledge enhances the understanding and natural knowledge of those who trust in Him (Daniel 1:17-20).

Even occult practitioners recognize that some knowledge can be revealed only by Spiritual means (Daniel 2:10-11). Although revealing Spiritual knowledge may bring honor to a person, ultimately the glory is to be directed to God (Daniel 2:46-47).

To reveal His power, glory, and sovereignty, God sometimes answers through a revelation far beyond anything we could have imagined (Habakkuk 1:5). God may provide knowledge of the far distant future, not only for the present or the immediate future, in order to test the faith of those who claim to trust Him.

As exemplified in Jesus' ministry

Even as a youth, Jesus exhibited a knowledge that far surpassed what He was expected to know at his age (Luke 2:46-47); he appeared to absorb human teaching with a Spiritually enriched understanding.

Although many people can guess others' attitudes and unvoiced opposition, Jesus knew people's thoughts with such precision that He could specifically and appropriately address every accusation or charge they thought of bringing against Him (Matthew 12:25-37). He had knowledge of things that were not discernible to the human mind—the thoughts and purposes in others' hearts and minds (Mark 2:8). Although it was not at all apparent to the other disciples, Jesus knew which of His followers did not truly believe, and He had always known the truth about Judas' eventual betrayal (John 6:64).

Jesus knew the unknowable—such as the miracle that God would perform in providing the Temple tax payment from a most unlikely source (Matthew 17:24-27), and the details of how it would be accomplished. He knew, even without seeing a situation first-hand, and despite the convictions of those who had, what God would be able to accomplish (Mark 5:39). It was apparent to the Jews that Jesus understood things that He could not have learned by human means. John 7:14-16 tells us that He was able to teach from a knowledge base far beyond what would normally have been expected of a man of His education. Jesus acknowledged that His knowledge was not from Himself but from God.

As illustrated in the New Testament

Even before his birth, John (the Baptist) was able to sense, through Spiritual knowledge, the nearness of the Savior (Luke 1:41-45). And his mother was given the knowledge to recognize the cause of his response. This is also a form of discernment. Elizabeth revealed a knowledge of Mary's child that had not yet been disclosed to her by human means.

In Acts 1:26, the disciples used the common practice of drawing lots to reveal God's selection of a replacement for Judas. This practice may have been much like the former use of the Urim and Thummim. After the day of Pentecost this practice was no longer mentioned in relation to the Church, presumably because the Holy Spirit could reveal His will directly to the people within whom He dwelt.

The Holy Spirit revealed to Stephen a visual assurance of his victory even as he died (Acts 7:55-56)—a knowledge he was able to share as encouragement to those who remained behind.

Philip allowed himself to be directed by knowledge from the

Holy Spirit (Acts 8:26-29). Because of Philip's obedience, he had the opportunity to teach the Ethiopian eunuch about Jesus.

Ananias was given specific knowledge of where to go and whom he should seek out (Acts 9:10-16). Although Ananias was afraid because he recognized whom the Lord meant, God was able to reassure him through further knowledge, and Ananias obeyed.

Spiritual knowledge is revealed to those who fear God and truly seek Him, not only to those who already know the gospel of salvation (Acts 10:1-6). It is because of Spiritual revelation that Cornelius sought out Peter, who would reveal to him the truth of the gospel.

Peter, too, needed the reassurance that Spiritual knowledge provided (Acts 10:19-20).

Spiritual knowledge can come through many channels. In Acts 27:23-26, an angel revealed part of God's plan to Paul as encouragement; the rest was apparently revealed more directly, as there is no mention of the angel's warning that the ship would run aground, although Paul revealed it to the sailors as being a necessary part of God's plan.

God provides visions and revelations in special circumstances as comfort or reassurance to certain people (2 Corinthians 12:1-6). Yet although the individual's heart responds, sometimes what is experienced is so different from our earthly experience that there is no way to describe it in earthly terms. Not all things are for general knowledge; God chooses to reveal to us only what we can understand. God reveals information to us according to His will and His timing (Ephesians 1:9-10). Sometimes He reveals mysteries that we could not otherwise understand (Ephesians 3:2-6). Paul knew not by intuition or circumstance but through Spiritual knowledge when his earthly death was imminent (2 Peter 1:13-15).

Related teachings

We now have access to the kind of Spiritual knowledge that comes directly from God and is revealed to us by the Holy Spirit.

Knowledge of the *glory of the Lord* is not a Spiritual gift but is revealed to all mankind through God's creation (Habakkuk 2:14). The Lord confides further in those who fear him (Psalm 25:14). He wants us to seek Him out and ask Him for understanding (Jeremiah 33:3). This is a common Spiritual knowledge that God provides to all who seek Him. God often speaks to us at night, when He doesn't compete with daily distractions for our attention (Psalm 16:7). Then we have quiet time to listen to him and consider what He is telling us.

God's purpose, through His revelation of knowledge, is to draw us closer to Him in trust (John 6:45). Our place, as believers, is to act on whatever knowledge He provides and trust Him with increasing certainty (Psalm 43:3). As we speak aloud, to others, the knowledge that God has revealed to our hearts, our own minds come to recognize what we did not previously understand (Psalm 49:3). Our understanding of whatever we think we know, in the natural, is limited; we can speak only from partial understanding. Only when God's holiness and purity of purpose clarify and complete our knowledge can we truly understand in depth (Psalm 73:15-17).

When we understand God's purposes, we are less likely to rebel or work at cross purposes against His plan, because then we recognize the fallacy of our own self-determined plans (Psalm 119:34). Those who trust in God's holiness recognize the superiority of His ways over their own (Psalm 119:66, 169). In fear, respect, and humility, wise people turn to God for answers they don't have in themselves (Proverbs 1:7). It is foolish to be content in our own knowledge and to not seek deeper understanding.

God disciplines us to renew our opportunities. When we respond positively, He can work within us and teach us directly; but when we remain obstinate and rebellious, we block Him out and He allows us to stumble along in our own muddling way (Proverbs 1:23). A wise person will ask God for deeper understanding rather than relying on human opinion or group consensus (Proverbs 15:14). Although there is a wealth of educated opinion and worldly experience available all around us, the few people who speak with God-given knowledge are of far more value to God's kingdom (Proverbs 20:15).

The Spiritual *gift* of knowledge is something more than the

Spiritual knowledge God provides to any who seek Him, or than the common knowledge of the glory of God that is revealed through creation to all mankind. It is the revelation (often, but not always, through prophecy) of specific details or circumstances that assist us in fulfilling God's purposes for His glory and the furtherance of His kingdom. It is counterfeited in occult practices, which we must not seek out or allow to seduce us away from God's ways (Leviticus 19:31). The false knowledge of cult doctrines and humanistic teachings can also be dangerously seductive (Proverbs 14:7; Romans 1:21-32; 1Timothy 6:20-21). We must be alert.

If we actively seek and respond to the knowledge God alone can provide, through His Word and through Spiritual gifts, He will provide whatever is appropriate (Proverbs 2:1-6).

It is to those who trust God's ways whom God entrusts with greater knowledge of His ways (Proverbs 3:31-32). God reveals Spiritual knowledge only to the limited degree that we can handle it and that it suits His purposes. God does not provide knowledge indiscriminately nor just because we may ask to know something (Acts 1:7). Neither should the knowledge that God entrusts to few be revealed indiscriminately, but it should be used with discretion (Proverbs 12:23). Misguided enthusiasm or impatience can lead us astray and cause more harm than good (Proverbs 19:2). A truly knowledgeable person speaks with restraint and self-control (Proverbs 17:27).

When Spiritual knowledge is revealed, it is to be acted upon, not ignored (Proverbs 13:16). We must be careful not to add our own embellishments and assumptions to the words that God gives us (Proverbs 30:5-6). Spiritual knowledge is perfect and powerful.

As Paul warned Timothy (1 Timothy 6:20-21) "Turn away from godless chatter and the opposing ideas of what is falsely called knowledge, which some have professed and in so doing have wandered from the faith."

Chapter 15

WISDOM

Definition: The special ability to achieve desired ends by effective means, following the guidance of the Holy Spirit

---

Scriptures cited in Chapter 15 – Wisdom

As a quality of God
Job 12:13
Psalm 104:10-19
Job 28:20-28
Job 32:8-9
Psalm 111:10
Psalm 51:6
Proverbs 8:1-21
Genesis 2:17

As illustrated in the Old Testament
Exodus 2:10
Exodus 33:12-17
Exodus. 2:11-15
Exodus 18:14-26
Deuteronomy 31:2-8, 23
Deuteronomy 34:9
Judges 6:14
Judges 6:15-40
Judges 7:1-8
Judges 8:10-12
Judges 8:22-23
Judges 8:24-27
2 Samuel 5:22-25
Judges 20:18, 23, 28
Judges 20:32-35
Daniel 2:14-19
2 Samuel 11:2-27
2 Samuel 15:31
2 Samuel 16:23
2 Samuel 17:14
2 Chronicles 24:17-22
1 Kings 3:5-7
1 Kings 3:8-12
1 Kings 3:13-14
1 Kings 12:6-15

1 Kings 12:26-33
1 Kings 3:5-14
2 Chronicles 9:22-23
Job 29:21-23

As exemplified in Jesus' ministry
Psalm 111:10
Luke 2:21-24, 39
Luke 2:40, 52
Luke 3:21-22
Luke 4:1-2
Luke 4:14-21
John 2:23-25
Matthew 13:10-15
Matthew 19:16-30
John 8:3-11

As illustrated in the New Testament
Acts 6:1-7
Acts 5:29-39
Acts 6:8-10
Psalm 119:98-100
Proverbs 21:30
Luke 7:29-30
Ecclesiastes 1:2-18
Ecclesiastes 7:12
Luke 6:47-49
Acts, ch. 27

Related teachings
Proverbs 14:12
Proverbs 3:7-8
Proverbs 8:35-36
Proverbs 13:10
Proverbs 15:33
Proverbs 14:33

Proverbs 8:1-21
Psalm 119:66
Proverbs 10:13-14
Psalm 37:30-31
Proverbs 17:28
Proverbs 15:7
Ecclesiastes 10:12
Proverbs 18:4;
Ecclesiastes 12:11
Proverbs 10:1, 23
Proverbs 15:21
Proverbs 19:11
Proverbs 29:8, 11
Proverbs 9:8-12
Proverbs 28:26
Proverbs 2:1-6
Proverbs 3:13-20
Proverbs 4:4-9
Proverbs 24:14
James 3:13-18
James 1:5-6
Colossians 1:9
Proverbs 24:3-4

Chapter 15
Wisdom

Definition: The special ability to achieve desired ends by effective means, following the guidance of the Holy Spirit

As a quality of God

It is often only when we find ourselves in extreme circumstances, when our understanding is at a loss, that many of us seek a wisdom beyond our own. We cannot find it within ourselves, nor in other created beings or objects, but only in the Creator and Designer of the universe and all that is in it (Job 12:13). For it was God who designed each species, who planned the interaction among all creation (Psalm 104:10-19). Only God is omniscient (Job 28:20-28). And God has provided, through the Holy Spirit, a means of allowing us to directly draw upon and benefit from aspects of His superior understanding (Job 32:8-9).

God wants us to humbly rely on His understanding (Psalm 111:10). It is in the nature of God to want to share His wisdom with us (Psalm 51:6). He gives us a desire for it and blesses those who act upon it (Proverbs 8:1-21). He does not want to grant us *carte blanche* of information and experience, which we would not be able to handle (Genesis 2:17), but He wants us to trust Him enough to apply the limited understanding that He gives us for specific purposes.

As illustrated in the Old Testament

Though raised as a grandson of an Egyptian Pharaoh (Exodus 2:10), Moses recognized that his own wisdom would be insufficient to lead the people of Israel out of the land of Egypt (Exodus 33:12-17). His previous attempts to protect the Israelites on the basis of his own wisdom had resulted in forty years of exile from Pharaoh's household (Exodus 2:11-15). Now he called upon God to accompany them, to teach him how to lead the nation of Israel out of Egypt. That humility and reliance upon God was the beginning of true wisdom. He was then also able to recognize and benefit from the wisdom of others (Exodus 18:14-26).

When Moses knew he was going to die, he transferred his leadership to Joshua (Deuteronomy 31:2-8, 23). Moses laid hands on Joshua and "Joshua the son of Nun was filled with the spirit of wisdom" (Deuteronomy 34:9).

Generations later, God called Gideon to defend Israel against Midian (Judges 6:14). Gideon knew that he could not rely on his own limited capabilities for such an assignment, so he humbled himself before God and sought multiple confirmations that he truly understood God's direction and that God would be faithful in bringing the victory (Judges 6:15-40). Human wisdom would have led Gideon to take as large an army as he could raise, but the Lord reduced the number to a few key men (Judges 7:1-8). Yet, this number was sufficient for the victory (Judges 8:10-12). And Gideon was wise enough to decline to rule over the Israelites as they requested but to leave their leadership to the Lord (Judges 8:22-23). Unfortunately, Gideon did not seek the Lord's wisdom in all such matters; when he allowed his own judgment to direct him, it caused trouble both for his family and for all Israel (Judges 8:24-27).

Use of Spiritual wisdom requires that we *seek* Spiritual wisdom (2 Samuel 5:22-25). Spiritual wisdom begins with inquiry into what the Lord wants us to do and how He wants us to accomplish it (as in Judges 20:18, 23, 28). It continues with faithfully obeying God, even in the face of apparent defeat (Judges 20:32-35).

Daniel also used wisdom both in enquiring about King Nebuchadnezzar's decree to destroy the wise men of Babylon and in recruiting the other Hebrews to intercede in prayer that he would be able to interpret the king's dream, and thereby ensure their own safety (Daniel 2:14-19).

As we see in Gideon, and in King David's life (2 Samuel 11:2-27), human—or false—wisdom is often used to cover or perpetuate sin. God can override this false wisdom with His own if we allow Him to.

Although King David knew that Ahithophel provided godly *sounding* advice, he recognized that it was human wisdom being used to undermine God's purposes. Therefore, he was able to ask the Lord to keep it from helping Absalom in his quest to overthrow God's anointed king (2 Samuel 15:31; 16:23; 17:14). Human wisdom can undermine our own efforts, as well as God's, and we are held accountable when we fail to respond to the Lord's correction (2 Chronicles 24:17-22).

We need to humble ourselves, recognizing that we lack wisdom, before we can seek the greater wisdom that God can provide (1 Kings 3:5-7). When we humbly seek God's wisdom to do the job our own cannot, He is faithful to provide it (1 Kings 3:8-12). And He gives us more than we ask for, not only to fulfill His purposes but as a blessing to us. The stipulation is that we continue to seek Him and not take those blessings for granted (1 Kings 3:13-14).

Compare this with the lack of wisdom found in 1 Kings 12:6-15, in which Rehoboam rejected the elders' advice; and with the worldly wisdom found in 1 Kings 12:26-33, in which Jehoboam raised idols to refocus the peoples' faith and loyalty. Both were sinful, and the leaders did not receive the Lord's support.

Solomon, on the other hand, humbled himself before the Lord, knowing, like Moses, that his own training and wisdom were insufficient to allow him to successfully lead the nation of Israel. God honored his request for help (1 Kings 3:5-14). As a result, Solomon became "greater in riches and wisdom than all the other kings of the earth. All the kings of the earth sought audience with Solomon to hear the wisdom God had put in his heart" (2 Chronicles 9:22-23).

When we have Spiritual wisdom, which comes only from maintaining open communication with the Lord, we can say with Job, "Men listened to me expectantly, waiting in silence for my counsel. After I had spoken, they spoke no more; my words fell gently on their ears. They waited for me as for showers and drank in my words as the spring rain" (Job 29:21-23).

As exemplified in Jesus' ministry

As the writer of Psalm 111:10 recognized, the fear of the Lord is the beginning of wisdom. Jesus' parents feared the Lord and followed his precepts (Luke 2:21-24, 39), wisely instilling that respect in the Son they had been given to raise (Luke 2:40, 52).

It is interesting to note that the grace of God was upon Jesus even before He was baptized in water, yet it was when He humbled Himself in baptism that He received clear affirmation of God's pleasure (Luke 3:21-22). Jesus then relied fully on the Holy Spirit to sustain Him and to supply His needs (Luke 4:1-2). His and God's mutual faithfulness reaffirmed in Him the empowerment of the Holy Spirit (Luke 4:14-21). Only then did He begin His active ministry.

Jesus used wisdom and discretion in selecting those to whom He would reveal Himself (John 2:23-25). He used wisdom in His teaching, as well, to fulfill prophecy (Matthew 13:10-15) and to reveal the hearts of people to themselves (Matthew 19:16-30; John 8:3-11).

As illustrated in the New Testament

As Moses had learned from his father-in-law Jethro, that even God-gifted leaders must rely on others to support and supplement their work, the apostles of the early Church used wisdom in delegating responsibility among the Christian disciples (Acts 6:1-7). They specified only two requirements in the delegates, that they be full of the Holy Spirit and that they exhibit wisdom.

We must not be misled into thinking that only believers can exhibit wisdom. God can provide wisdom to nonbelievers in order to protect His people and advance His purposes (Acts 5:29-39). But Spiritual wisdom is far superior (Acts 6:8-10; Psalm 119:98-100; Proverbs 21:30; Luke 7:29-30). Wisdom is pointless in itself unless it is given a purpose (Ecclesiastes 1:2-18; Ecclesiastes 7:12); but Spiritual wisdom is not given without a God-directed purpose, for which we are held responsible (Luke 6:47-49).

The Apostle Paul used Spiritual wisdom in conjunction with the gifts of knowledge and prophecy in chapter 27 of Acts, through his warnings regarding the danger of the sailing, loosing the lifeboat to keep the crew onboard, and, despite the imminent peril of shipwreck, encouraging all on board to maintain their strength by eating adequately.

Related teachings

We have a choice: whether to be content in our foolishness or to seek wisdom (Proverbs 14:12; Proverbs 3:7-8; Proverbs 8:35-36). Yet, even in choosing wisdom, we need to take it seriously (Proverbs 14:6, 8)—to fear the Lord (Proverbs 1:7) and humble ourselves before Him (Proverbs 13:10; 15:33). God gives us enough wisdom to know that we must choose (Proverbs 14:33), but that choice is ours to make (Proverbs 8:1-21). We can continue in darkness, or we can pray, like the writer of Psalm 119 (v. 66), "Teach me knowledge and good judgment, for I believe in your commands."

Our choice is revealed every time we open our mouths to speak (Proverbs 10:13-14; Psalm 37:30-31; Proverbs 17:28; Proverbs 15:7; Ecclesiastes 10:12; Proverbs 18:4; Ecclesiastes 12:11). And it is revealed in our behavior (Proverbs 10:1, 23; Proverbs 15:21; Proverbs 19:11; Proverbs 29:8, 11). Like Jesus, we must use wisdom and discretion when we are dealing with others (Proverbs 9:8-12). We must recognize and strive to overcome our own tendencies toward foolishness (Proverbs 28:26; Proverbs 2:1-6) and remember the benefits God pours out on those who rely on His wisdom (Proverbs 3:13-20, Proverbs 4:4-9; Proverbs 24:14).

Words to the wise: "Who is wise and understanding among you? Let him show it by his good life, by deeds done in the humility that comes from wisdom. But if you harbor bitter envy and selfish ambition in your hearts, do not boast about it or deny the truth. Such 'wisdom' does not come down from heaven but is earthly, unspiritual, of the devil. For where you have envy and selfish ambition, there you find disorder and every evil practice. But the wisdom that comes from heaven is first of all pure; then peace-loving, considerate, submissive, full of mercy and good fruit, impartial and sincere. Peacemakers who sow in peace raise a harvest of righteousness" (James 3:13-18)."If any of you lacks wisdom, he should ask God, who gives generously to all without finding fault, and it will be given to him. But when he asks, he must believe and not doubt, because he who doubts is like a wave of the sea, blown and tossed by the wind" (James 1:5-6).

As is true with other Spiritual gifts, it is important that those with the particular gift of Spiritual wisdom be supported in prayer by the rest of the Church (Colossians 1:9), because the use of this gift, in particular, in conjunction with any other, enhances the value of both (Proverbs 24:3-4).

Chapter 16

DISCERNMENT

Definition: The special ability to accurately identify the source and nature of a spirit or motivation

---

Scriptures cited in Chapter 16 – Discernment

As a quality of God
1 Samuel 2:3
Psalm 7:9
Psalm 139:2-4
Jeremiah 17:10

As illustrated in the Old Testament
Ezra 2:63
Leviticus 8:8
Exodus 28:30
Judges 2:18-19
Judges 6:34
Judges 6:34-40
Judges 7:2-15
1 Samuel 6-12
1 Samuel 17:28
1 Samuel 25:33
2 Samuel 12:1-14
2 Samuel 14:17-18
2 Samuel 11:2-4
2 Samuel 24:2, 10
2 Samuel 13:5-7
1 Kings 3:9-12
1 Kings 4:29
1 Kings 3:23-27

As exemplified in Jesus' ministry
John 8:15-16
Luke 4:33-35
Matthew 16:23

As illustrated in the New Testament
Acts 5:1-4
Acts 16:16-18
1 Corinthians 2:11-14

Related teachings
Hebrews 4:12-13
1 Corinthians 4:4-5
1 John 4:1-5
Psalm 14:12
Psalm 16:25
1 John 4:6
Hebrews 5:14
Proverbs 2:3-6
John 7:24
John 8:50

Chapter 16

Discernment

Definition: The special ability to accurately identify the source and nature of a spirit or motivation

As a quality of God

God is able to judge us because He knows what is in our hearts, the motivation for our actions, and our intent. Hannah recognized this in 1 Samuel 2:3, when she acknowledged that God weighs our actions. In Psalm 7:9, David expresses a similar understanding that God searches hearts and minds. David also sang, "You know when I sit and when I rise; you perceive my thoughts from afar. You discern my going out and my lying down; you are familiar with all my ways. Before a word is on my tongue you know it completely, O Lord." (Psalm 139:2-4).

These statements are confirmed in Jeremiah 17:10, when God Himself says, "I the Lord search the heart and examine the mind, to reward a man according to his conduct, according to what his deeds deserve."

As illustrated in the Old Testament

Although direct Spiritual discernment is noticeably absent throughout the Old Testament. God provided insight to Old Testament believers in other ways.

Priests relied on the Urim and Thummim, which were stored in the ephod, their priestly garments. The Urim and Thummim were somewhat like dice, which would be cast to determine God's will. Examples of this practice can be found in Ezra 2:63 and Leviticus 8:8. It is also referred to in Exodus 28:30. Hence, King David often called for the ephod to be brought before him when he faced a major decision.

It is unclear how God directly assisted the anointed judges to make wise judgments, but it is clear that without Godly guidance the nation quickly reverted to sin (Judges 2:18-19). Judges 6:34 indicates that "the Spirit of the Lord came upon Gideon," but whether it was for discernment or some other short-term purpose, we can't be certain.

Outward signs were another method of discernment used for making judgments (Judges 6:34-40; 7:2-15). Gideon, seeking the Lord's truth, conscientiously asked for outward signs to confirm that he was making the correct decisions.

Discernment was often closely aligned with prophecy and Spiritual knowledge, as illustrated in 1 Samuel 6-12. When God guided the selection of David from among his brothers, despite David's absence from the gathering, He warned Samuel to overlook outward appearances and to look beyond the circumstances of David's absence, assuring him that God could see beyond the surface appearance, into the heart. (*False* discernment, on the other hand, such as that seen in 1 Samuel 17:28, is often based on arrogance, envy, or intentional deception, not on truth.)

God often used messengers—prophets, angels, and others—to provide enlightenment. Abigail's discernment of David's integrity was based on human observation of his character (1 Samuel 25:33). Nathan's rebuke of David (2 Samuel 12:1-14) was through a word of knowledge and prophecy.

Although the woman from Tekoa declared that King David's judgment was "like the angel of God in discerning good and evil" (2 Samuel 14:17-18), David's judgment frequently proved faulty when it was based on selfishness (2 Samuel 11:2-4), arrogance (2 Samuel 24:2, 10), or deception from others (2 Samuel 13:5-7) rather than on Spiritual revelation.

1 Kings 3:9-12; 4:29, Solomon requested wisdom and discernment, which God granted, giving him wisdom, great insight, and a wide breadth of understanding. Yet his discernment appears to have been based less on Spiritual discernment than on Spiritual wisdom and understanding of human nature. Solomon relied less on Spiritual discernment to make his judgment in 1 Kings 3:23-27, than on Spiritual wisdom to know how to set up a situation from which he could determine the truth of the child's true parentage.

As exemplified in Jesus' ministry

Jesus pointed out to the judgmental Pharisees that they were judging Him by human standards but that He wasn't passing judgment on anyone. Any judgment that He would make would be in accordance with the Father's judgment (John 8:15-16).

Jesus was able to discern the difference, in Luke 4:33-35, between the spirit—the demon—and the man it had possessed and was therefore able to confront it and order it to leave the man.

Jesus rebuked Peter for rejecting out of hand His prophecy of His approaching suffering and death in Jerusalem (Matthew 16:23). It is clear that Jesus recognized that Satan was using Peter's human concern to raise a stumbling block for Him, yet he pointed out that Satan was able to do so only because Peter was not putting God's interests first and hence was unable to perceive that God might have a greater purpose to achieve through the forthcoming sufferings.

As illustrated in the New Testament

The gift of discernment appears in the New Testament Church to have been exercised primarily when there was a fine line, difficult to distinguish by human means, between acceptable behavior and unacceptable motivation. When Ananias attempted to deceive the apostles in Acts 5:1-4, the Holy Spirit revealed the truth to Peter, who confronted Ananias about the deception. It would not have been wrong for Ananias to have kept some of the sale price of his property for himself; what was wrong was that he lied to God by trying to make the Church believe he was giving them all he had received for the land.

At first glance or initial hearing, the declaration by the slave girl in Acts 16:16-18 wouldn't seem to be demonic. It was, in fact, the truth. As her declarations continued, however, Paul became troubled, sensing that something was wrong in the *way* she was declaring the truth. Perhaps it was because she was focusing attention on them instead of on Jesus. Paul recognized the demonic influence despite its outward appearance. As soon as it was confronted, the demonic spirit left her.

Each time a demon or satanic motivation was discerned, it was also boldly confronted. This facet of the gift of discernment was often used in conjunction with the gifted ability to drive out spirits.

The Apostle Paul wrote to the Corinthians (1 Corinthians 2:11-14), "For who among men knows the thoughts of a man except the man's spirit within him? In the same way no one knows the thoughts of God except the Spirit of God. We have not received the spirit of the world but the Spirit who is from God, that we may understand what God has freely given us. This is what we speak, not in words taught us by human wisdom but in words taught by the Spirit, expressing spiritual truths in spiritual words. The man without the Spirit does not accept the things that come from the Spirit of God, for they are foolishness to him, and he cannot understand them, because they are spiritually discerned."

Related teachings

The word of God judges the thoughts and intentions of the heart (Hebrews 4:12-13), not to hold up a measuring tape so we can judge others, but so we can recognize and acknowledge the truth of our own sinful nature. As Paul continued in his letter to the Corinthians (1 Corinthians 4:4-5), "My conscience is clear, but that does not make me innocent. It is the Lord who judges me. Therefore judge nothing before the appointed time; wait till the Lord comes. He will bring to light what is hidden in darkness and will expose the motives of men's hearts. At that time each will receive his praise from God."

The Apostle John wrote that we must test the spirits to see whether they are from God (1 John 4:1-5). A spirit that acknowledges that Jesus Christ has come in the flesh is from God; any spirit that will not acknowledge Jesus is not from God. This is the spirit of the antichrist, speaking from the viewpoint of the world. It will be accepted by the general public but is not from God. A warning in this regard is provided in both Psalm 14:12 and Psalm 16:25: "There is a way that seems right to a man, but in the end it leads to death."

People who know God on a personal basis recognize the Spirit of truth—the reflection of God's own character—and can discern its counterfeit (1 John 4:6). But those whose faith is still immature need to be taught so their faith will be bolstered and their understanding of God's character will increase so they can become more Spiritually discerning (Hebrews 5:14).

As Solomon wrote in Proverbs 3-6, "If you call out for insight and cry aloud for understanding, and if you look for it as for silver and search for it as for hidden treasure, then you will understand the fear of the Lord and find the knowledge of God. For the Lord gives wisdom, and from His mouth come knowledge and understanding."

"Stop judging from mere appearances, and make a right judgment" (John 7:24).

As with use of all the Spiritual gifts, the credit must go to God, not to ourselves. Even Jesus said, "I am not seeking glory for myself, but there is One who seeks it, and He is the judge" (John 8:50).

Chapter 17

FAITH

Definition: The special ability to express an extraordinary level of faith in such a way as to inspire others to greater faith in Christ

---

Scriptures cited in Chapter 17 – Faith

As a quality of God
Hebrews 11:1
Genesis 1:1-31
Jeremiah 29:11
Hebrews 11:6
1 John 5:14-15

As illustrated in the Old Testament
1 Samuel 17
1 Samuel 17:32-52
Nehemiah 2:11-18
Nehemiah 2:1-9

As exemplified in Jesus' ministry
John 8:28-30
John 11:4-44
Matthew 26:56
Luke 8:22-25
Luke 10:18

As illustrated in the New Testament
Luke 7:2-10
Philippians 1:20-28
2 Corinthians 4:13-18
2 Corinthians 5:1-9

Related teachings
Matthew 21:19-22
Romans 1:21-23
James 2:17
Galatians 3:2-5
James 2:18

Chapter 17
Faith

> *Definition: The special ability to express an extraordinary level of faith in such a way as to inspire others to greater faith in Christ*

As a quality of God

It might seem odd to say that faith is a quality of God. For why would God need to exercise faith? Hebrews 11:1 says that "faith is being sure of what we hope for and certain of what we do not see." God is omniscient—He knows all; He sees all—so perhaps it would be better to say that the quality of God we are actually looking at is certainty, the epitome of faith.

Genesis 1:1-31 illustrates for us how God exercised faith: He envisioned what was to be, commanded it to be, created it according to His vision, and declared it good.

"'For I know the plans I have for you,' declares the LORD" (in Jeremiah 29:11), "'plans to prosper you and not to harm you, plans to give you hope and a future.'" Although we, whose knowledge and sight are limited, must exercise faith to hold onto the hope God offers us for our future, God knows the future and can be certain of it. He does not need faith as we do because, to Him, the future is already sure. It is His assurance to us of what He knows and what He sees in the future that inspires our faith.

Hebrews 11:6 explains that "without faith it is impossible to please God, because anyone who comes to Him must believe that He exists and that He rewards those who earnestly seek Him." If we don't believe He exists, our faith will have nothing to inspire it—literally, to "breathe life" into it—and any eternal hope we might have will be in vain.

By contrast, God commends those who express faith in Him, thus encouraging and inspiring us to continue to exercise our faith. God offers additional assurance that He will meet any request that is in agreement with His desires and purposes (1 John 5:14-15), thereby further inspiring the faith of those who trust in Him.

As illustrated in the Old Testament

The story of David, in 1 Samuel 17, illustrates the gift of faith. David found his confidence strengthened as he recounted past victories to King Saul, recognizing that the Lord would be in the forthcoming battle with Goliath just as He had been in David's previous confrontations with the lion and the bear (1 Samuel 17:32-52). David chose to rely not on the protection devised by man, which felt to him to be awkward and unmanageable, but chose to rely instead on the proven armor of his faith in God. David's physical weapons were not a match for Goliath's, but his Spiritual weaponry proved far superior. His faith and subsequent defeat of Goliath bolstered the morale of Saul's entire army. God's ultimate purpose through David's faith was to display for the soldiers of both sides that it was the Lord's battle and therefore the Lord's victory (v. 47).

In a similar way, Nehemiah did not feel a need to seek confirmation from Jerusalem's officials of what he knew God had called him to do (Nehemiah 2:11-18). God had already granted him favor with King Artaxerxes (Nehemiah 2:1-9), but Nehemiah understood that the local officials would not necessarily share his certainty in the outcome. Only after he had assessed the conditions he would be facing did he approach the officials with his plan so that he could discuss it with them knowledgeably and give them confidence in his understanding of the situation. Nehemiah's faith in his ability to accomplish the task under God's blessing and guidance, already evidenced in the king's having granted his blessing, gave the officials faith to approve the work.

Both of these examples illustrate believers' faith, honored and strengthened by God, witnessing to other people of the Lord's faithfulness.

As exemplified in Jesus' ministry

Jesus exemplifies pure faith. As Son of God, He had full access to whatever the Father chose to reveal to Him, and He acted on it accordingly. It was Jesus' utter reliance on the Father to know what to say and what to do in any given situation that caused others to put their faith in Him (John 8:28-30). He was a direct and always-true connection between the people and God the Father. When the Jews discovered that the prophecies of His sacrificial crucifixion were true, many more came to believe in Him just as they believed in the Father.

In John 11:4-44, Jesus expressed His own faith, regarding Lazarus's recovery, to offer assurance to His friends. He also explained the reason for Lazarus's illness, though they could not understand it at that time. It did not seem reasonable to anyone else for Jesus to have waited so long before going to Lazarus, but Jesus had a purpose for waiting.

Despite the Jews' previous attempt to stone Jesus, He expressed faith in His purpose and that He would be protected through the earthly lifetime allotted Him (vv. 7-16). Jesus expressed both His knowledge of the circumstances and His faith in the outcome to bolster the disciples' faith, expressing a sense of satisfaction in the situation that would give them an opportunity to increase their faith. Thomas, in particular, must have been something of a pessimist, not at all sure that Jesus—and the rest of them—would not be stoned. Yet he was among those whose faith Jesus wanted to encourage.

Lazarus's sister Martha, the assertive sister, the "do-er" of the family, took action to go meet Jesus. With a very normal expression of grief, she expressed both anger and blame even as she expressed her faith in Jesus. Although she professed faith—"I know"—, that faith in her knowledge was limited. Even when Jesus assured her that her brother would rise again, she found it difficult to believe that He meant "today, in this present world." Jesus reassured her, putting specific words to what she believed, and encouraging her to confirm this herself, thereby reinforcing her faith (vv. 20-32). Mary was less assertive than her sister, yet eager for Jesus' familiar and comforting presence. Although her grief, like her sister's, poured out of her in accusation, her faith was expressed in humility as she fell at his feet.

Jesus wept, I believe, not because Lazarus had died but because He was moved by the distress Mary and the others felt over their loss (vv. 33-40). The people, too, expressed their simultaneous grief, frustration, and faith. Touched by their spiritual confusion, He was moved to take action to strengthen their faltering faith. He cares when our faith wavers, and He takes steps to steady it. Jesus reassured the ever-practical Martha to reinforce her faith.

When Jesus prayed his thanks to the Father aloud (vv. 41-44), it served to reinforce the faith of the other mourners. It also provides us with a pattern of prayer, thanksgiving, affirmation that God has heard our cries for help, and encouragement for the sake of bolstering the observers' faith. God does His part when He calls us to an act of faith; but we must do our parts as well, not only to express our faith, to offer our sincere thanks, but also to accept His provision. We must have the faith to "remove the grave clothes"—to *act* on what God has done, in cooperation with Him.

Jesus rarely seemed hurried when called to restore the health of someone on the deathbed or to raise those who had already died. Jesus' delays provided opportunities for Him to exercise far greater miracles than He might otherwise have done, thereby enhancing His disciples' understanding of God's grace and restoration power (Matthew 26:56).

In Luke 8:22-25, Jesus identified a destination, expressing certainty that they would reach it. When His disciples refocused on the wind and waves, Jesus rebuked all evidence that deterred them and encouraged His followers to exercise their faith that they would indeed reach their goal.

Luke 10:18 tells us that, as the apostles were casting out spirits, Jesus was visualizing Satan's fall from heaven. As it had done when He calmed the storm on Lake Genneseret (the Sea of Galilee), His faith in the results strengthened the faith and understanding of those He was training.

As illustrated in the New Testament

A centurion exhibited the gift of faith when he approached Jesus to heal his servant (Luke 7:2-10). The centurion, in humility, recognized that he deserved nothing. Instead, he focused Jesus' attention on the servant. It was with this unselfish attitude that the centurion sought Jesus' help. He recognized Jesus' authority and acknowledged that His word would suffice as well as His physical presence could. Jesus honored the centurion's faith and took the opportunity to use his expression of faith to encourage the crowd.

Paul wrote of his faith in order to encourage and equip the churches he loved (Philippians 1:20-28). He openly told of his many troubles to contrast them with his faith in the God of grace who sustained him throughout his trials (2 Corinthians 4:13-18). He knew that his life on earth, with its accompanying troubles, was temporary and would eventually be destroyed; but he was also certain that his eternal life would be far better and that God's Spirit—His presence here in this temporal life—was only a foretaste of what we will enjoy in eternity. So he made it his goal to please God in all things, looking always toward his eternal reward, rather than seeking relief from his temporary sufferings which, through grace, were serving to enrich his appreciation for and relationship with the Lord (2 Corinthians 5:1-9).

Related teachings

Jesus taught a multi-layered lesson when He withered the unfruitful fig tree (Matthew 21:19-22). The fig tree was showy in its thick foliage, but it produced nothing of value. Although there were leaves to maintain its own vigor, there was no fruit to retain moisture, to nourish and support life outside the tree itself, and there was no seed for reproduction. The tree was like a self-centered, self-satisfied believer who isolates himself from the needs around him (Romans 1:21-23). Our faith comes from the Lord, but, as James says, "faith by itself, if it is not accompanied by action, is dead" (James 2:17). Because the tree was fruitless—like a believer without works—Jesus removed His life-sustaining power from the tree, causing it to wither.

While encouraging His disciples to be useful and warning them that unless their faith bore fruit, it, like the tree, would quickly atrophy and die, Jesus was also teaching them that, by applying their faith to God's purposes, it would be strengthened toward trusting Him to do whatever needed to be done. As we exercise our faith, it is strengthened; if we ignore it, it atrophies. So it is in our best interest, as well as the interest of the Church as a whole, to use what faith we have, to respond to God's guidance with expectancy in His faithfulness. This encourages those around us, and it encourages us, in the future, to rely to an even greater extent on God.

Deeds never take the place of faith; any deeds not motivated by faith, though they may be of earthly benefit, can never be enough to compensate for our sins (Galatians 3:2-5). God expects us to act on our faith, not merely profess it in theory. He values the faith that motivates the deeds more than He values the deeds themselves (James 2:18).

Chapter 18

GIVING

Definition: The special ability to give generously and joyfully of one's time or material goods without considering it loss

---

Scriptures cited in Chapter 18 – Giving

As a quality of God
Psalm 136:25
Psalm 112:9
Psalm 36:7-9
2 Corinthians 10-12
2 Corinthians 9:8

Acts 22:44-45
Acts 4:32
Acts 5:1-4
Proverbs 28:25
2 Thessalonians 3:6-14

As illustrated in the Old Testament
Exodus 25:1-7
Exodus 35:21-29
Exodus 32:2-4
1 Chronicles 29:1-9
2 Chronicles 24:8-11

Related teachings
Matthew 6:19-21
1Timothy 6:17-19
Hebrews 13:5
2 Corinthians 9:6-15
Malachi 3:10
1 John 3:17
2 Corinthians 8:7
2 Corinthians 8:12
Hebrews 13:15-16

As exemplified in Jesus' ministry
Matthew 6:19-21
Luke 12:32-34
Luke 9:58
Mark 6:8-9
Matthew 5:40-48
Proverbs 21:14
Matthew 9:35-38
Matthew 14:15-21
Matthew 15:32-38
Matthew 20:34
Mark 1:41-42

As illustrated in the New Testament
Acts 3:2-7
John 12:1-8
Acts 10:1-4
Acts 11:29-30
Acts 20:34-35
2 Corinthians 8:2-5

Chapter 18
Giving

> *Definition: The special ability to give generously and joyfully of one's time or material goods without considering it loss*

As a quality of God

God freely provides food for every creature (Psalm 136:25). His own giving is an example for us: He gives generously to the poor without expecting anything in return (Psalm 112:9). Psalm 36:7-9 acknowledges "How priceless is your unfailing love! Both high and low among men find refuge in the shadow of your wings. They feast on the abundance of your house; you give them drink from your river of delights. For with You is the fountain of life; in your light we see light."

God provides the initial resources from which we give (2 Corinthians 10-12). As he sees our faithfulness in giving, He can increase our resources so that the amount and quality of our giving can increase. We are blessed; the needs of His people are met; and He, too, reaps a generous return for His giving in the form of a greater harvest of thanksgiving to Him.

Giving involves more than money. God's grace toward us is so abundant that we are supplied more than enough to offer it to others (2 Corinthians 9:8).

As illustrated in the Old Testament

When God requested Moses to collect an offering from the Israelites (Exodus 25:1-7), notice that it was according to how each man's heart prompted him to give. The offering could be in any of a number of forms, including precious metals, fibers for weaving, animal hides, fine wood, olive oil, spices, and gemstones. Additional freewill offerings collected later (Exodus 35:21-29) included skilled craftsmanship (v 26).

Again, "everyone who was willing and whose heart moved him came and brought an offering to the Lord" (v.21).

Compare these freewill offerings with Aaron's command to "take off the gold earrings that your wives, your sons and your daughters are wearing, and bring them to me" (Exodus 32:2-4). This "gifting" was not from the heart and became the basis for idolatry.

Inspired giving inspires further giving; generosity inspires generosity, as we see in 1 Chronicles 29:1-9. As an example, 2 Chronicles 24:8-11 indicates that when a collection chest was made to collect taxes to repair the desecrated Temple, contributions were brought "gladly" until the chest was full. The chest was emptied regularly and returned to its place so a large amount of money was collected, as needed for the Temple's repairs.

As exemplified in Jesus' ministry

Jesus taught in Matthew 6:19-21 and Luke 12:32-34 not to cling to earthly possessions but to use them to help the poor and, in that way, to make no-risk investments in heaven. It is apparent that He lived this way Himself, when we see that He warned a would-be follower (Luke 9:58) that He lived without many personal possessions beyond the clothes on His back, or even a house of His own. By relying wholly on God's provision for His needs, Jesus could devote Himself to a life of itinerant teaching and ministry, traveling wherever the Holy Spirit led Him. He taught His disciples to do the same in Mark 6:8-9.

He taught us to be generous by offering more than is asked or expected (Matthew 5:40-48).

Addressing both physical and spiritual needs generously encourages the good and helps to placate those bent on evil, which can turn away their wrath (Proverbs 21:14). We are to extend God's love and grace to them, being "perfect...as your heavenly Father is perfect" (Matthew 5:48).

He taught us in Matthew 9:35-38 to pray for what is needed to serve God's purposes. God will provide. When we use what is available, with sincere appreciation, God provides more than a sufficiency. This is exemplified in Matthew 14:15-21 and Matthew 15:32-38.

As well as providing food, Jesus' compassionate giving also included healing (Matthew 20:34 and Mark 1:41-42) and the use of other Spiritual gifts as directed by the Holy Spirit.

As illustrated in the New Testament

Our giving is not limited to material goods but is also available in the form of Spiritual gifts and service, as we see in Acts 3:2-7. Even beyond the hospitality that Mary and Martha offered (John 12:1-8), and despite Judas's criticism, Mary contributed in an extravagant way to bless Jesus.

Heart-felt giving, like that of Cornelius in Acts 10:1-4, does not go unnoticed by the Lord.

Generosity encourages others and blesses the properly motivated giver as much as the recipient. (Acts 11:29-30; Acts 20:34-35). The Macedonian churches gave generously, despite their own poverty (2 Corinthians 8:2-5), to send support for the needy believers in Jerusalem. They gave not only to the limit of their financial ability, but beyond it because of the joy they received in helping others. Paul had expected less, but they were committed to serving the Lord first and foremost. And, though it was a financial hardship to them, they considered it a joy to support Paul as well. God enables us to give beyond our natural ability, if we allow Him to.

In Acts 22:44-45, we see that the believers were together and shared everything in common, selling their possessions to provide for anyone who had need. United in purpose and commitment to one another, this communal means of support generally worked well, as we see again in Acts 4:32. However, note that in Acts 5:1-4, selfishness and deceit came into play, illustrating for us the principle given in Proverbs 28:25, that although those who trusted in the Lord had prospered, the spirits of greed, envy, and competition threatened to stir up dissension. As a precaution, to ensure that no one was taken unfair advantage of, Paul wrote to the Thessalonians (2 Thessalonians 3:6-14), "if anyone is not willing to work, then he is not to eat, either."

Related teachings

Matthew 6:19-21 gives us a way to identify our own values. We will protect and cling to whatever we value most. If it is money, we will be slow to give it up; if it is time, we will be hesitant to make time-consuming commitments; if it is acts of faith and spiritual obedience, we will seek out opportunities so we can add more to our storehouse in heaven, placing the earthly cost in a secondary position of importance.

In Paul's first letter to Timothy (1Timothy 6:17-19), he warned that the wealthy are not to be arrogant nor to put their hope in wealth, but to put their hope in God, to be rich in good deeds, and to be generous and willing to share, thereby gaining a truer perspective on "life that is truly life."

Hebrews 13:5 also teaches us to keep our lives free from the love of money and be content with what we have, remembering that God has said He will provide for us and for our needs.

In 2 Corinthians 9:6-15 we are given the principle of sowing and reaping. It applies not only to seed and money, but to all our resources. Notice the importance of attitude (v. 7). God can give us all we need, and more, in every way, to enhance our ability to continue our good work (v. 8), through which we honor Him—the ultimate purpose of all our gifts (v. 13). A side benefit that faithful givers accrue is the appreciative prayer support from the beneficiaries. Ultimately, all thanks should be directed to God.

This principle is applicable not only to money but to all areas … serving, using gifts, and more. It is the only area where God has actually encouraged us to test Him to verify the validity of the promise (Malachi 3:10).

Scripture challenges us:

"If anyone has material possessions and sees his brother in need but has no pity on him, how can the love of God be in him?" (1 John 3:17).

"But just as you excel in everything—in faith, in speech, in knowledge, in complete earnestness and in your love for us—see that you also excel in this grace of giving" (2 Corinthians 8:7).

At the same time, we are assured that "if the willingness is there, the gift is acceptable according to what one has, not according to what he does not have" (2 Corinthians 8:12).

Hebrews 13:15-16 reiterates, "Through Jesus, therefore, let us continually offer to God a sacrifice of praise—the fruit of lips that confess his name. And do not forget to do good and to share with others, for with such sacrifices God is pleased."

Chapter 19

POVERTY

Definition: The special ability to eschew the comforts associated with material wealth, and to trust in God's provision, as witness of His manifested care

---

Scriptures cited in Chapter 19 – Poverty

As a quality of God
Deuteronomy 28:12-13
Isaiah 33:6

As illustrated in the Old Testament
Ezekiel 44:28-30
Psalm 34:9-10
Proverbs 11:28
Psalm 33:18-19
1 Kings 17:1-6

As exemplified in Jesus' ministry
Luke 12:22-31
Luke 9:57-10:1
Mark 12:13-17
Matthew 17:24-18:1

As illustrated in the New Testament
Matthew 6:25-27
Luke 22:35-37
Galatians 2:10
1 Timothy 6:6-12
Philippians 4:12-13

Related teachings
Hebrews 13:5
Proverbs 16:16

Chapter 19
Poverty

Definition: The special ability to eschew the comforts associated with material wealth, and to trust in God's provision, as witness of His manifested care

As a quality of God

Although it would be difficult to say that God is impoverished, we can unequivocally say that He does not cling to material wealth for His own comfort but distributes it generously to those who trust in His provision.

Deuteronomy 28:12-13 tells us "The LORD will open the heavens, the storehouse of his bounty, to send rain on your land in season and to bless all the work of your hands."

Similarly, Isaiah 33:6 says, "He will be the sure foundation for your times, a rich store of salvation and wisdom and knowledge; the fear of the LORD is the key to this treasure."

As illustrated in the Old Testament

Some people are called by God to a life of dependence on the Lord's provision, as He did the priests in Ezekiel 44:28-30. Although this is not a mandate to support all the world's poor, God's people have a responsibility to support those whom God has specifically called to this position. Assistance to the poor beyond this specific responsibility is a matter of free-will giving.

Those who put their faith in the Lord are more secure than those who trust in material wealth, earthly power or human strength (Psalm 34:9-10; Proverbs 11:28). We see the promise of Psalm 33:18-19 carried out in 1 Kings 17:1-6, when He provided for Elijah through the famine.

As exemplified in Jesus' ministry

Jesus Himself chose a life of poverty (Luke 12:22-31). He apparently did not maintain a household of His own. He traveled almost continuously so probably owned little more than the clothes He wore day after day. He gleaned grain from the fields He passed along the roadside. Yet He was well provided for. He was a frequent and welcome guest in various households, only rarely lacked human companionship or fellowship with God and repeatedly showed the disciples how God could provide not only for their small number but for overwhelming crowds of people with only minimal worldly provisions. We can see again in Luke 9:57-10:1 that Jesus exemplified a willingness to commit to poverty for the sake of ministering to others.

Despite his earthly poverty, Jesus recognized that we have and should meet our financial obligations to the government as well as to God (Mark 12:13-17). He relied on God's provision to pay the Temple tax (Matthew 17:24-18:1) even though, as God's Son, He was technically exempt. He paid the tax to avoid becoming a stumbling block to those who were not exempt, and to avoid causing offense that would hinder His ministry, using God's provision to pay Peter's portion of the tax as well as His own.

As illustrated in the New Testament

Jesus told his disciples, in Matthew 6:25-27, to be unconcerned about what they would eat or drink or wear because God would provide just as surely for them as He does for the rest of His creation.

Jesus recognized that there is a time and place to eschew material possessions but also a time for appropriate purchasing power (Luke 22:35-37), for which one might have to forfeit personal comfort.

The Holy Spirit puts on the hearts of His servants a desire to meet the needs of the poor, as we see in Galatians 2:10, so we can trust in Him to provide.

Paul's letter to Timothy (1 Timothy 6:6-12) reminds us that there is nothing inherently wrong with wealth. Our focus should be not on achieving either wealth or poverty but on striving for godliness. Paul learned to be content in a wide variety of circumstances, from wealth to poverty, from freedom to imprisonment, from health to chronic physical problems, from a position of political honor to that of a political prisoner. Through it all his goal was godliness, not wealth. God gives us reason to feel compassion for others—often by calling us to similar circumstances for a season, during which times He meets our needs to develop our faith in Him, as we can see in Paul's letter to the Philippians (Philippians 4:12-13).

Related teachings

We are reminded in Hebrews 13:5 to "keep [our] lives free from the love of money and be content with what [we] have, because God has said, 'Never will I leave you; never will I forsake you.'"

Whereas those who have material wealth tend to place their faith in their wealth; those without material wealth tend to rely more on God. Material goods cannot impart wisdom and understanding (Proverbs 16:16). Only God can provide them. This close dependence on the Lord is the goal of those who choose a life of voluntary poverty through the power and leading of the Holy Spirit.

Chapter 20

PHYSICAL POWER

Definition: The application of an extraordinary physical trait or ability, as provided and directed by the Holy Spirit, for a specific purpose

---

Scriptures cited in Chapter 20 – Physical Power

As a quality of God
Genesis 1:1
Psalm 149:4
Psalm 65:6

As illustrated in the Old Testament
Genesis 5:24
Hebrews 11:5
2 Kings 2:11
1 King 18:46
Judges 13:3-16:30
Numbers 6:2-4
Esther 2:15
Esther 2:8-17
Esther 7:2-8:11
1 Samuel 17: 37-50
1 Samuel 17:37

As exemplified in Jesus' ministry
Luke 4:1-14
Matthew 4:12
Acts 8:39
Matthew 14: 25-31
Matthew 14:29-31
Genesis 5:24
2 Kings 2:11
Mark 16:19
Luke 24:51

As illustrated in the New Testament
Mark 16:17-18
Luke 10:19-20
2 Corinthians 12:9-10

Related teachings
Psalm 147:10
Psalm 18:32-39
Acts 8:39
Exodus 14:21
Hebrews 12:1-3
1 Corinthians 9:24-25
Psalm 21:13

Chapter 20

Physical Power

> *Definition: The application of an extraordinary physical trait or ability, as provided and directed by the Holy Spirit, for a specific purpose*

As a quality of God

The Spirit of God created a physical environment for physical beings for His own pleasure (Genesis 1:1; Psalm 149:4). We can see one example of the strength and power of God Himself in Psalm 65:6, which acknowledges Him as the one "who formed the mountains by your power, having armed yourself with strength."

As illustrated in the Old Testament

Unlike most of humanity, Enoch did not taste of death but was called directly from his earthly life into heaven by God (Genesis 5:24; Hebrews 11:5). Elijah, too, was taken up in a whirlwind to heaven (2 Kings 2:11). These are miraculous examples of physical displacement contrary to the known laws of physics. Yet we will see similar events occur in both the life of Jesus and in the New Testament Church.

We read in 1 King 18:46, another incident in which the power of the Lord came upon Elijah. Although King Ahab was driving a chariot hard to outrace a storm that was already upon him, Elijah was able to outrun Ahab's horses, demonstrating apparently superhuman strength, speed, and endurance.

More familiar stories of physical prowess are related in the story of Samson, who was born a Nazirite, dedicated before birth to God (Judges 13:3-16:30). Notice that when the Spirit of the Lord came upon him in power, Samson exhibited superhuman strength and stamina. This remarkable strength was a hallmark of Samson's life, but always when the Holy Spirit was with him. When his head was shaved—a violation of the Nazirite vow (Numbers 6:2-4)—he could no longer draw on the Lord's power and was left vulnerable, as are all who leave the Lord's protective power.

Another physical attribute that the Lord was able to use for His purposes was Esther's beauty, as we read in the book of Esther. Although there is no direct reference to the Holy Spirit's intervention, aside from her apparently winning character (Esther 2:15), her physical beauty in conjunction with Godly counsel helped ensure the king's favor so he was willing to hear her petitions, which ultimately saved her people (Esther 2:8-17; Esther 7:2-8:11).

Once again, we read in 1 Samuel 17:37-50 the story of a man who trusted in God's deliverance against seemingly overwhelming odds, as David faced down Goliath with minimal weaponry, saying "The Lord who delivered me from the paw of the lion and from the paw of the bear will deliver me from the hand of this Philistine" (1 Samuel 17:37).

As exemplified in Jesus' ministry

Jesus exhibited great physical endurance in the face of extreme deprivation and temptation, as we see in Luke 4:1-14. Having eaten nothing during the forty days in the desert following His baptism, "He was hungry." He drew on God's Word repeatedly in response to the devil's tempting suggestions. After the devil had left Him, Jesus heard of John's imprisonment, so returned to Galilee (Matthew 4:12). Whether He was relying on the strength of the Holy Spirit as he walked, or was returned in a manner similar to what we will soon see in Acts 8:39, in which Philip was miraculously transported by the Spirit of the Lord to another location, is not indicated. We are merely told that "Jesus returned to Galilee in the power of the Spirit" (Luke 4:12).

Other examples of miraculous physical displacement that challenge the known laws of physics appear in Matthew 14:25-31, when Jesus walked on the water toward the disciples' boat on the Sea of Galilee, and a few verses later when He called Peter to walk across the water to Him from the boat (Matthew 14:29-31). Peter was empowered by obedience to the call of Christ, but when he lost confidence, he began to sink. Jesus immediately reached out to him and returned with him to the boat.

Much as Enoch was called directly into heaven (Genesis 5:24), and Elijah, in his chariot, was taken up to heaven in a whirlwind (2 Kings 2:11), both Mark 16:19 and Luke 24:51 record that Jesus also ascended bodily, directly into heaven, following His resurrection from the dead and His subsequent days on earth.

As illustrated in the New Testament

When Jesus commissioned His disciples (Mark 16:17-18), He granted them the ability to drive out demons, speak in new tongues, pick up snakes with their hands, suffer no ill effects from drinking deadly poison, and be able to place their hands on sick people to make them well. He said further to the followers He sent out in pairs (Luke 10:19-20) that He gave them authority to "trample on snakes and scorpions and to overcome all the power of the enemy." These promises were borne out in Acts 28:3-5 when "a viper, driven out by the heat, fastened itself on [Paul's] hand. … But Paul shook the snake off into the fire and suffered no ill effects."

As mentioned previously, Philip experienced physical displacement when "the Spirit of the Lord caught away Philip" (Acts 8:39, KJV) and he found himself in Azatus (current-day Ashdod) after he had baptized the Ethiopian eunuch along the desert road that ran between Jerusalem and Gaza.

Although we do not see physical power manifested in the New Testament in quite the same ways that we did in the Old Testament, we do see it used as a compliment or component of other gifts, most notably in the Spiritual gift of martyrdom. Since the Holy Spirit has come to dwell within the hearts of believers, we can draw directly on His power. His strength is greatest when we recognize and acknowledge our personal weakness (2 Corinthians 12:9-10). In this way it is He who is glorified instead of the person through whom His power is manifested. Much as Jesus had done on the cross, when Stephen was being stoned to death (Acts 7:59-60), his remarkable fortitude enabled him to focus not on his pain but on the Holy Spirit, extending forgiveness even during the attack.

Related teachings

Psalm 147:10 tells us that God's "pleasure is not in the strength of the horse, nor his delight in the legs of a man; the LORD delights in those who fear him, who put their hope in His unfailing love."

As David sang in Psalm 18:32-39, God gives us strength. He guides our feet. He trains us, placing us in circumstances ahead of time that will prepare us physically and mentally for the tasks ahead. Verses 35 and 36 acknowledge, "You give me your shield of victory, and your right hand sustains me; you stoop down to make me great. You broaden the path beneath me, so that my ankles do not turn." These elements can be taken figuratively, of course, but they can sometimes be literal as well. As a father might put out a hand to keep something from hitting his child, God shields us from forces that we don't see. Does He actually make a path for us broader? Why not? Don't we clear shrubbery away from the sides of a walkway if it poses a hazard to those passing by? God does the same for us, both figuratively and, on occasion, literally, as he opened the passage through the Red Sea for Moses and the Israelites (Exodus 14:21). Notice that although David was the victor in the battle of which he sang, he acknowledges that the victory was not from his own ability but from God.

Athletes often use their public exposure to call attention to their favorite causes or to act as spokespeople for businesses. Athletes who have been specially gifted with extraordinary stamina or other physical abilities by the Holy Spirit have an even greater opportunity to be effective as spokespersons for Him when they allow God to fully direct both their public and private lives and activities (Hebrews 12:1-3). Athletic prizes and awards are momentarily gratifying, but the eternal prize is worth a lifetime of sustained effort (1 Corinthians 9:24-25).

David reminds us again, in Psalm 21:13, that when the Holy Spirit enables us, the glory belongs to the Lord.

Chapter 21

CELIBACY

Definition: The special ability that allows a person to eschew sexual desires to concentrate on Spiritual matters

---

Scriptures cited in Chapter 21 – Celibacy

As a quality of God
Genesis 3:22-24
Luke 1:26-37
Genesis 1:1-2

As illustrated in the Old Testament
Jeremiah 16:1-4

As exemplified in Jesus' ministry
Matthew 27:55
Hebrews 4:15

As illustrated in the New Testament
Genesis 1:27-28
Psalm 127:3
1 Corinthians 7:1-9

Related teachings
1 Corinthians 7:32-35
Matthew 19:8-12
Matthew 22:30
Psalm 103:20-21
Revelation 19:7

Celibacy

Definition: The special ability that allows a person to eschew sexual desires to concentrate on Spiritual matters

As a quality of God

God is holy. As the Creator, He formed Adam and Eve through asexual means. Too soon, sin spawned a separation between fallen humanity and the purity that is God (Genesis 3:22-24). God needed to provide a human savior, His own Son, who would exhibit the character of the heavenly Father. The Father accomplished it by producing a child in the womb of a human woman, fathered by the Holy Spirit. Mary was still a virgin when she conceived Jesus, as the power of the Holy Spirit overshadowed her (Luke 1:26-37), creating Jesus within her in much the same way that the Holy Spirit had moved over the face of the deep (Genesis 1:1-2) to bring form to the earth and to all that was yet to be created. God achieved His purpose while maintaining His pure and holy separation from humanity's sinful nature.

As illustrated in the Old Testament

The prophet Jeremiah was called to practice celibacy as long as he remained in exile from Israel. God called him to a form of His own holiness, to be set apart from the corrupting influences of a foreign culture. God may choose to call His people to remain celibate for a specified and limited time, through a specific situation, or for an entire lifetime (Jeremiah 16:1-4). The gift of celibacy is His way of empowering people to fulfill that call without feeling overwhelming and detracting sexual temptation.

As exemplified in Jesus' ministry

We can see the evidence of celibacy in Jesus' life. Because many women were stepping in to fill the housekeeping role for Jesus as he traveled from place to place, it is evident that He had not established a marital relationship with any one woman who would have taken on that role for Him (Matthew 27:55). Although Jesus understood the sexual temptation women could have over men, He was able to overcome the urgings of his own human nature. Apparently He found it possible to refocus His mind to keep his thoughts pure (see Hebrews 4:15), to overcome any temptations of lust, and to remain faithful to His Spiritual mission.

As illustrated in the New Testament

We can't expect everyone to be empowered to remain celibate unless it is in the will and purpose of God that they should do so. Obviously it is not His will that everyone should, since He created Adam and Eve, male and female, and told them to "be fruitful and multiply and replenish the earth" (Genesis 1:27-28). Psalm 127:3 reminds us that "sons are a heritage from the Lord, children a reward from him." So the marital relationship is obviously sanctioned and blessed by God. But even married people can observe "fasting" times of celibacy for specific Spiritual purposes (1 Corinthians 7:1-9). It appears, from this passage (v. 7), that, for the sake of his ministry, Paul was among those who experienced the gift of celibacy.

Related teachings

As the Apostle Paul observed, when we are in a close relationship with another person, our concern is to please that person and to maintain the closeness of that relationship. We spend considerable time thinking about and doing things for the other person. This can distract us from focusing on spiritual business. The purpose of celibacy is to avoid the emotional distractions that intimate physical relationships produce so that, instead, we can form the closest possible relationship with God (1 Corinthians 7:32-35).

Jesus acknowledged that some people are born without an option to exercise their sexuality. Mankind himself denies the option to others. Yet others, like Jesus Himself, make a conscious choice to eschew it for a holy purpose. God chooses to whom He will give special gifting to remain celibate (Matthew 19:8-12).

Matthew 22:30 appears to indicate that the angels are celibate. Like the angels, with no need to reproduce, our resurrection bodies will have spiritual purposes that will have no need for sexuality. Our purpose, like that of the angels, will be to continually draw closer in our relationship with the Lord and to do His will (Psalm 103:20-21). The focus of that eternal relationship with the Lord becomes clear when we see that it is likened to a marriage (Revelation 19:7).

Chapter 22

MARTYRDOM

Definition: The special ability to witness through one's own life or, especially, through one's death, as the ultimate statement of faith

---

Scriptures cited in Chapter 22 – Martyrdom

As a quality of God
John 17:5
John 3:16
Isaiah 53:10-12

As illustrated in the Old Testament
Deuteronomy 32:35-36, 43
Judges, chs. 13-16
Judges 16:25-30
2 Chronicles 24:20
Job 19:23
Genesis 37-48
Genesis 45:8
Genesis 50:26
Ezekiel 24:15-24
Daniel 3:14-29
Hosea 1-3
Jonah 1:9-16
Jonah 3:1-5

As exemplified in Jesus' ministry
John 16:19-23
Luke 18:31-33
Luke 22:41-44
John 12:24-25
Mark 15:1-5
John 19:6-11
John 19:11
Luke 23:33-34
John 19:12, 19-22
Luke 23:39-43
Mark 15:39

As illustrated in the New Testament
Luke 9:23-25
2 Chronicles 24:20
Acts 7:57-60
John 1: 6-8
Luke 7:26-28
Malachi 3:1
Mark 6:17-28
Luke 1:13-17
Luke 1:39-44
Matthew 3:13
John 1:19-34
John 21:19
Acts 20:22-24
Acts 21:10-15
Acts 9:24-25
Acts 14:19-20
Acts 16:22-40
John 21:19
Acts 20:22-24
1 Timothy 6:12
Ephesians 6:11-12

Related teachings
Luke 9:23
Romans 12:9-21
John 15: 1-8
John 15:6
Luke 9:23-25
Ephesians 5:25-30
1 Peter 3:1-2
Ephesians 6:5-8
1 Peter 2:18-21
James 4:11-12

Romans 13:1-2
Psalm 4:17
Psalm 56:4
Psalm 66:8-12
John 12:24
Psalm 73:24
Psalm 116:15
Psalm 118:17
Proverbs 14:32
Proverbs 20:22
Isaiah 57:1-2
Jeremiah 1: 19
John 15:12-13
2 Corinthians 4:10-12
Philippians 1:12-14
Philippians 1:20
1 John 3:16

Martyrdom

Definition: The special ability to witness through one's own life or, especially, through one's death, as the ultimate statement of faith

As a quality of God

God is eternal—the Father cannot die—but He can sacrifice and suffer loss. The triune God witnessed to the world in the person of Jesus, His Son. It was Jesus who left the comfort and glory of heaven (John 17:5) to abide with sin-filled humanity and to give His life for the salvation of any who would believe in Him (John 3:16). Through His life He exemplified, as a witness to humanity, what a holy and perfectly faithful relationship with God could be; through His death He made that relationship with God possible for mankind (Isaiah 53:10-12).

As illustrated in the Old Testament

Throughout the Old Testament, God called individuals to forego comforts, sacrifice personal wellbeing, and risk their lives to accomplish specific tasks for Him. They were imperfect but faith-filled people who knew that they acted under the Lord's authority and that recompense, both for themselves and for any who wronged them (Deuteronomy 32:35-36, 43), belonged to Him.

Among these were Samson, who was called from the time of his conception to be set apart for God's service (Judges, chs. 13-16). He died with the Philistines upon whom he carried out God's vengeance (Judges 16:25-30).

Another example is Jehoiada the priest, whom the Holy Spirit directed to call the people to account; he was stoned to death for his obedience to God, and called upon the Lord to add his death to their account (2 Chronicles 24:20).

Job remained steadfast and relied on his God (Job 19:23) even though he didn't understand the reasons behind his suffering. Job's recorded experiences remind us even today that God is still sovereign, even when we do not see or understand His purposes.

Without initially recognizing the purposes behind it, Joseph (Genesis 37-48) remained faithful to God while suffering separation from his family, slavery, unjust accusation, and long-term imprisonment. He eventually came to realize that it was God who had positioned him in Egypt to accomplish His purposes there (Genesis 45:8).

Like Job and Joseph (Genesis 50:26) mentioned above, Ezekiel (Ezekiel 24:15-24), Daniel (Daniel 3:14-29), Hosea (Hosea 1-3), Jonah (Jonah 1:9-16; Jonah 3:1-5), and others did not die martyrs' deaths but lived martyrs' lives, exemplifying God's messages to the people, and standing as living witnesses of God's faithfulness.

As exemplified in Jesus' ministry

It was during Jesus' martyrdom that the attitude of vengeance and retribution by the martyr, which had prevailed through much of the Old Testament, changed. Jesus knew the purpose of His forthcoming sufferings (John 16:19-23). He recognized the kind of suffering that lay ahead of Him (Luke 18:31-33), and neither sought nor desired it, and even asked to be spared if the result could be accomplished in any other way (Luke 22:41-44). It could not be (John 12:24-25).

He did not try to talk His way out of it (Mark 15:1-5). Jesus did not seek retribution on those who persecuted Him. He went so far as to absolve Pilate of his guilt in the trial (John 19:6-11).

Jesus' commitment and reliance on God, which was evident throughout His trial and suffering, bore witness to His faith and righteousness. He maintained an attitude of grace and forgiveness (John 19:11; Luke 23:33-34). Pilate recognized it (John 19:12, 19-22), one of the criminals who were crucified with Him recognized it (Luke 23:39-43), as did the centurion at the cross (Mark 15:39).

As illustrated in the New Testament

A general Christian teaching about daily martyrdom is found in Luke 9:23-25. However, empowerment by the Holy Spirit, through the *gift* of martyrdom, results in an even more powerful and effective witness.

Notice the difference in attitude between the final words of Zechariah, as he was stoned to death (2 Chronicles 24:20) and of Stephen, who suffered the same fate as a follower of Christ (Acts 7:57-60). One sought vengeance; the other expressed forgiveness.

The first martyr revealed in the New Testament, John the Baptist (John 1: 6-8), began his witness even before his birth. Jesus Himself testified that John was the fulfillment of Old Testament prophecy (Luke 7:26-28; Malachi 3:1), sent for the specific purpose of witnessing to the coming of Christ. Although John was killed because of his exhortation to King Herod (Mark 6:17-28), it was his preceding life that witnessed most strongly of Jesus as Christ. Luke 1:13-17 tells of the prophecy before his conception of what his role would be for the Lord and that he would be filled with the Holy Spirit while still in the womb. Indeed, the fulfillment of that prophecy became apparent with his prenatal witness to his mother of Jesus' impending birth (Luke 1:39-44). John continued, as he preached and baptized, to listen to the Lord's direction; he sought Jesus' own permission before acting on His request for baptism (Matthew 3:13). He gave a strong and effective testimony of Jesus Christ (John 1:19-34).

When Jesus appeared to Peter, following his own crucifixion and resurrection, He prepared Peter by alerting him to the manner of death he too would face (John 21:19), concluding simply with the direction, "Follow me!"

In Acts 20:22-24, Paul clearly expressed the attitude of one with the gift of martyrdom: "And now, compelled by the Spirit, I am going to Jerusalem, not knowing what will happen to me there. I only know that in every city the Holy Spirit warns me that prison and hardships are facing me. However, I consider my life worth nothing to me, if only I may finish the race and complete the task the Lord Jesus has given me – the task of testifying to the gospel of God's grace." When

Paul's foreknowledge through the Holy Spirit was confirmed through prophecy (Acts 21:10-15), his companions tried to dissuade him from continuing to Jerusalem. Paul reiterated his determination to go: "Why are you weeping and breaking my heart? I am ready not only to be bound, but also to die in Jerusalem for the name of the Lord Jesus."

Notice, however, in Acts 9:24-25, Acts 14:19-20, and Acts 16:22-40, that Paul knew when to flee a threat and when to submit. The Holy Spirit helped him discern his course of action each time. Because of his Spiritual gift, he also discerned God's greater purpose for the trials he faced. Unless we have received specific prophecy, word of knowledge, or a clear, Spiritually expressed direction, such as those found in John 21:19 or Acts 20:22-24, we are expected to continue to "fight the good fight," as Paul called it (1 Timothy 6:12), resisting the devil (Ephesians 6:11-12) and maintaining our faith that we will be allowed to complete the course the Lord has set before us. Even when he knew from the Holy Spirit that he faced arrest, imprisonment, and more, Paul utilized the legal channels available to him to obtain reprieves when he could.

Related teachings

Martyrdom is not merely suffering with patience or in silence. Neither is it necessarily to the death. Rather, it is accepting specific sufferings or sacrifice as a necessary part of God's design to advance His plans. A narrow humanistic view states that "the guy who dies never wins." When we have eternity in view, however, we see that those who reap the greatest reward are those who have made the greatest sacrifice in accordance with God's will. Daily self-denial and recommitment to Christ that He calls us to in Luke 9:23 is a form of martyrdom, witnessing to the transformative power of the gospel.

But empowerment by the Holy Spirit, through the *gift* of martyrdom, results in an even more powerful and effective witness. We may be called as martyrs to a limited extent, or for a limited time, in what seems to be an insignificant situation (though no one's salvation is insignificant to God) or to make a greater sacrifice for a greater glory.

Our submissive attitude under Christ's authority is crucial, whatever the circumstances may be (Romans 12:9-21).

As believers, to become increasingly fruitful, we should expect to be pruned (John 15:1-8). Pruning is painful, but the alternative is to be cut off as an unproductive branch and be burned (John 15:6).

I am convinced that more people have the gift of martyrdom than we normally recognize. Martyrdom is a lifestyle-witness, an attitude witness that cannot be faked. All of us are called to a life of witnessing to the unsaved people around us (Luke 9:23-25): husbands (Ephesians 5:25-30) or wives (1 Peter 3:1-2), unreasonably demanding bosses (Ephesians 6:5-8; 1 Peter 2:18-21), less-than-ideal neighbors (James 4:11-12), questionable leadership (Romans 13:1-2), and so on.

As we read Psalm 4:17; Psalm 56:4; Psalm 66:8-12; and John 12:24, we see that the martyr's calling is to be willing to suffer for the higher purpose God has for our lives. We also know that God is with us through our suffering (Psalm 73:24; Psalm 116:15; Psalm 118:17; Proverbs 14:32; Proverbs 20:22; Isaiah 57:1-2; Jeremiah 1:19) and our reward at the other end is great.

As we are called to witness throughout the world, the Holy Spirit empowers us to love one another just as Christ loved us (John 15:12-13), whether it is through our lives and sufferings or by expressing the love of Christ through our deaths (2 Corinthians 4:10-12; Philippians 1:12-14; Philippians 1:20; 1 John 3:16).

Chapter 23

HELPS

Definition: The special ability to protect or assist others in a gracious manner to allow them to exercise their own Spiritual gifts and callings

---

Scriptures cited in Chapter 23 – Helps

As a quality of God
Genesis 2:18-20
Genesis 20-22 (KJV)
Psalm 121:2-8
Deuteronomy 33:29
Psalm 10:14
Psalm 46:1
Hebrews 13:6

As illustrated in the Old Testament
Exodus 17:8-11
Exodus 17:12
Ruth 2:5-9, 12-13
2 Chronicles 22:11-12
1 Kings 18:4
Ezra 1:5-6
Psalm 63:7
Jeremiah 36:4-8

As exemplified in Jesus' ministry
Mark 9:16-29
Luke 5:1-11
Luke 7:24-28
Hebrews 5:7-9
John 14:16-18

As illustrated in the New Testament
Acts 9:22-25
Acts 13:2-5
1 Peter 5:12
1 Peter 1:1

Related teachings
Isaiah 63:5-6
Hosea 13:9
Luke 10:38-42
1 Samuel 30:21
Acts 26:22
John 5:7-15

Helps

> *Definition: The special ability to protect or assist others in a gracious manner to allow them to exercise their own Spiritual gifts and callings*

As a quality of God

God recognized from the beginning that humanity requires help appropriate for our unique needs (Genesis 2:18-20). He met the need for Adam by providing a helper "meet" (suitable) for him (Genesis 20-22, KJV).

God also recognizes that, living as we are now in a fallen world, we need help beyond what the limitations of humanity can provide. He provides that help Himself (Psalm 121:2-8). His help is available not only to nations (Deuteronomy 33:29) but to individuals as well (Psalm 10:14).

Just as the sons of Korah acknowledged that God is a very present help in trouble (Psalm 46:1), the writer of Hebrews wrote that, as believers in Christ, we can say with confidence, "The Lord is my helper" (Hebrews 13:6).

As illustrated in the Old Testament

By holding the staff of God up high, Moses helped the Hebrew warriors as they fought the Amalekites, serving as an encourager and a rallying point to them (Exodus 17:8-11), a visible point of contact with God's overcoming power. When Moses began to tire, Aaron and Hur served as helpers to him so that he could continue in his own helping role (Exodus 17:12).

Ruth was committed to serving her mother-in-law Naomi, working to provide their food. Boaz, a distant relative of the women's dead husbands, took interest in her as she gleaned the leftovers from his fields (Ruth 2:5-9, 12-13). He helped her by providing his protection as she worked and by offering her access to his prepared water supply for her comfort as she continued in her efforts.

2 Chronicles 22:11-12 tells of Jehosheba, who protected her nephew Joash from certain death when the other royal princes were being murdered by Athaliah; Joash would eventually become one of the more Godly kings of Judah.

Obadiah helped the Lord's prophets by protecting them and supplying their provisions while they were in hiding from Jezebel (1 Kings 18:4).

Sometimes God inspired people to help by providing building materials and supplies that others needed to accomplish their tasks (Ezra 1:5-6).

Through his help, God provides comfort and encouragement (Psalm 63:7). The help He gives through obedient followers eases the way for those He has called to a task. In Jeremiah 36:4-8, Baruch helped not only by writing down Jeremiah's words, but by filling in for Jeremiah in reading the words to the people.

As exemplified in Jesus' ministry

Jesus helped the afflicted boy, in Mark 9:16-29, by casting out the spirit that His disciples had been unable to; He helped the disciples by explaining why they had been unable to accomplish the task ("only by prayer" – with God's help). They appear to have attempted to cast out the spirit by their own authority rather than by God's. He also helped the boy's father by reinforcing his faith.

Luke 5:1-11 recounts that Jesus used his assistance to intrigue Simon, to encourage and persuade him that, with Jesus' help, his efforts would be productive.

Jesus acknowledged John the Baptist's invaluable role as His own helper who prepared the way before Him (Luke 7:24-28). John lived humbly, spent his life preparing the way for Someone else, and would eventually be beheaded. Yet Jesus said, "among those born of women there is no one greater than John."

Jesus spent his entire ministry helping others come to know God the Father, helping them overcome their human weaknesses, and helping them learn to reach others to do the same. His greatest role as helper was ultimately in helping us all to reconcile our sinful natures to God by providing the means of salvation through the sacrifice of His human life, meeting requirements of holiness that no sin-marred human would have been capable of providing (Hebrews 5:7-9).

When His earthly ministry was nearing its end, Jesus promised to provide another "Counselor" (Helper) whose time with us would be unlimited (John 14:16-18). Jesus was the human manifestation of God's Spirit of Truth. Following His bodily ascension to the Father, His Holy Spirit returned to be with all believers to remain with us permanently as a Helper, Comforter, and Counselor.

As illustrated in the New Testament

When Paul was being sought by the city authorities, the other believers, whom Paul had been teaching, helped him escape so that he could continue his ministry in other cities (Acts 9:22-25).

Although it was Barnabas and Saul who had been called to the mission in Cyprus (Acts 13:2-5), the Apostle John accompanied them as an assistant so they could focus their efforts on the work to which they had been specifically called.

Though Silas's assistance in acting as Peter's scribe (1 Peter 5:12) may seem of little importance to those of us who take easy and rapid dissemination of information for granted, without his help Peter would have been unable to send encouragement and guidance "to God's elect, strangers in the world, scattered throughout Pontus, Galatia, Cappadocia, Asia and Bithynia" (1 Peter 1:1). Nor would we be able to read his words today.

Related teachings

Failure to help when God requires it of us does not leave Him helpless but incurs His wrath toward us (Isaiah 63:5-6). Even His people are not exempt from His wrath when we reject and defy him (Hosea 13:9).

Yet we must judge where and when to provide help; it isn't always called for, even in situations that appear to demand it, as we see in Luke 10:38-42. Unless we are directed by the Holy Spirit to help, the Lord may have higher priorities.

Although help often seems insignificant to those either on the sidelines or playing a more central role, it is often vital to the overall effort; helpers should share in any benefits of their efforts' outcome (1 Samuel 30:21).

We have a responsibility to acknowledge and appreciate the help we receive, whether directly from God (Acts 26:22) or from people (John 5:7-15), not taking its far-reaching value for granted.

Chapter 24

SERVICE

Definition: The special ability to benefit others by one's assistance, labor, and compassionate care

---

Scriptures cited in Chapter 24 – Service

As a quality of God
Deuteronomy 20:18
Ephesians 4:11

As illustrated in the Old Testament
Ruth 2:17-18
Nehemiah 5:14-18

As exemplified in Jesus' ministry
Matthew 20:28
Matthew 8:5-8, 13
Luke 9:48

As illustrated in the New Testament
Acts 16:25-34
Acts 6:1-6

Related teachings
Proverbs 31:10-20
Galatians 1:10
Hebrews 13:1-3
1 Peter 4:10-11
1 Corinthians 16:15-18
2 Corinthians 9:12-14

Chapter 24
Service

Definition: The special ability to benefit others by one's assistance, labor, and compassionate care[3]

As a quality of God

We see the gift of service in action by God Himself when we read Deuteronomy 20:18. He defends widows and orphans; and he provides succor to those who feel alienated, meeting their basic survival needs when they have no other recourse. Ephesians 4:11 reminds us that it was the Holy Spirit who provided the Spiritual gifts to prepare believers to serve and build up one another and thus strengthen the Church in faith and unity of purpose. In this way, the Holy Spirit was providing His assistance and compassionate care to us as individuals and as a Church body.

As illustrated in the OT

This kind of service of beneficence appears throughout the Old Testament. Ruth, for instance, provided manual labor to support and care for her mother-in-law Naomi (Ruth 2:17-18). Nehemiah, too, made a point of minimizing his financial burden on others; instead, he conscientiously strove to provide generously for the needs of those in his jurisdiction, both those in the public eye and foreigners who came from a distance (Nehemiah 5:14-18).

As exemplified in Jesus' ministry

Jesus lived a life of service to others, not demanding to be served (Matthew 20:28).

In Matthew 8:5-8, 13, the centurion, asking Jesus to heal his

---

[3] Definition is based on the Greek "*diakoneo*" as used in 1 Peter 4:11.

servant, recognized the hierarchy of authority, and considered himself unworthy to have Jesus under his roof.

Christ's attitude toward service to others is shown in Luke 9:48— that someone considered the least important is treated as the most important by God; by treating a child, for instance, as tenderly as God would, we magnify God's love and grace.

As illustrated in the NT

Acts 16:25-34 is an example of reciprocated service. Paul and Silas served the jailer; then the jailer served them; in the process, all were blessed. As with all Spiritual gifts, the purpose of the gift of service is to bring praise and thanksgiving to God.

Acts 6:1-6 illustrates how this kind of service was applied in the early Church. The twelve apostles served the Church by delegating responsibilities according to the Spiritual gifts needed to perform specific duties. Those delegated served the Church by carrying out their assigned responsibilities. In this way all the needs of the Church were met without overburdening anyone.

Related teachings

The Spiritual gift of service can be manifested in everyday situations, in the home (Proverbs 31:10-20) as well as in the public arena. The purpose is not to win the approval of men but to be obedient to God (Galatians 1:10). In Hebrews 13:1-3, we are admonished to love one another as siblings, to entertain strangers, and to have compassion on those who are suffering and in prison. 1 Peter 4:10 calls us to use whatever gifts we have to serve others by faithfully extending God's grace in whatever ways those gifts have prepared us to do, remembering that our work is merely an extension of God's grace, so that the glory and praise for the services we do belong to Him.

Yet it would be wrong to overlook those who act in obedience to God's call to serve. Paul wrote in 1 Corinthians 16:15-18 that we should cooperate with those who participate in the work of service and that their efforts deserve to be recognized. Paul was careful to recognize such service himself, as, in 2 Corinthians 9:12-14, he acknowledged the Corinthian church for supplying the needs of God's people, sharing generously with others, and otherwise extending God's grace in material ways.

Chapter 25

SERVITUDE

---

*Definition: The special ability to humble oneself
in obedience and service as directed by others*

Scriptures cited in Chapter 25 – Servitude

As a quality of God
John 16:13

As illustrated in the Old Testament
1 Samuel 17:15-22
1 Samuel 18:5
1 Samuel 20:4
1 Samuel 14:6-7
1 King 19:15-21

As exemplified in Jesus' ministry
John 13:3-17
John 15:10, 20
John 17:4

As illustrated in the New Testament
Acts 9:10-17
1 Corinthians 9:19-23
Acts 20:22-23
Acts 8:26-38

Related teachings
Acts 13:22
1 Samuel 16:1-5
Ephesians 6:5-8
Ephesians 6:6
Galatians 1:10

Chapter 25
Servitude

Definition: The special ability to humble oneself in obedience and service as directed by others[4]

As a quality of God

The Holy Spirit, speaking not on His own initiative but as a representative of the Father, is shown in John 16:13 to humble Himself in obedience and service to Another.

As illustrated in the Old Testament

This attitude of humility in servitude was demonstrated in David's willingness to serve both his father, Jesse (1 Samuel 17:15-22), and King Saul (1 Samuel 18:5). Saul's son Jonathan exhibited a similar willingness when he told David, "Whatever you want me to do, I'll do for you" (1 Samuel 20:4). And when Jonathan proposed approaching the enemy, Jonathan's armor bearer, likewise, showed a similar willingness to serve in whatever way he was needed (1 Samuel 14:6-7).

In 1 King 19:15-21, Elijah was obedient as a servant of the Lord. When he called Elisha to assist and learn from him, Elisha was willing to humble himself to both serve and be taught by Elijah. Yet feeling responsibilities to his dependents, Elisha asked some leniency and patience so he could take care of matters at home; Elijah did not demand immediate allegiance but he expressed humility as a mentor also, remembering his own position of servitude to God.

---

[4] Definition is based on the Greek "*duelo*"—servant.

As exemplified in Jesus' ministry

Jesus, while knowing that all things were subject to Him, exemplified, in John 13:3-17, the humility of a servant to those who called him their Teacher, whom the world might have reasonably expected to serve Him. He did not demand exaltation but chose to set an example of servitude toward those who were learning from him, teaching them to express a similar attitude of service and humility toward one another (v. 14).

In John 15:10, He voiced the concept clearly, that His followers are expected to live in obedience to Him, just as He had always lived in obedience to the Father. He reminded them in verse 20 of the same chapter that, as His representatives, they should expect to be treated no better nor be accepted any less than He, their Master, had been.

Jesus acknowledged, in John 17:4, that His purpose in accomplishing the work He had been given to do was to bring glory to His heavenly Father.

As illustrated in the New Testament

Ananias was willing, even in the face of a great perceived risk, to serve God's purpose for him by seeking out Saul of Tarsus in Damascus (Acts 9:10-17). In voicing his fears to God, he received reassurance and encouragement before proceeding.

Paul, also, though he considered himself free from Jewish law, was willing to subject himself to the laws of those he wanted to win for Christ. He explained in 1 Corinthians 9:19-23, that he humbled himself as a servant for the sake of winning souls for the Lord.

Even when he received forewarning instead of reassurance about what awaited him, Paul, "compelled by the Spirit," was obedient in his servitude (Acts 20:22-23).

Philip showed humility in servitude when the Holy Spirit directed him to make himself available to the Ethiopian eunuch who was puzzling over scripture as he traveled (Acts 8:26-38).

Related teachings

By testifying about David's attitude of servitude, as recorded in Acts 13:22, "I have found David son of Jesse a man after my own heart; he will do everything I want him to do," God provided a standard by which we can measure our own attitude. Are we willing to do everything God wants us to do? 1 Samuel 16:1-5 again illustrates that it is all right to seek clarification and reassurance in how to proceed.

That high standard of obedience is reinforced for us in Ephesians 6:5-8, when Paul reminds us, as slaves, that everything we do should be done as servants of Christ, in submission to His will and His direction, with humility. Both Ephesians 6:6 and Galatians 1:10 emphasize the importance of sincerity, submitting not as men-pleasers but doing God's will from the heart, keeping in mind Who it is we serve.

Chapter 26

HOSPITALITY

Definition: The special ability to address the physical and emotional needs of others in such a way that they feel comfortable and valued

---

Scriptures cited in Chapter 26 – Hospitality

As a quality of God
Genesis 2:15-18

As illustrated in the Old Testament
Leviticus 19:33-34
Joshua 2:1-15
Proverbs 25:21-22
Matthew 5:43-48
2 John 1:7-11

As exemplified in Jesus' ministry
John 8:13-21
John 15:32-38

As illustrated in the New Testament
Luke 10:38-42
Acts 9:26-28

Related teachings
Matthew 10:11-15
Matthew 10:11-14
Luke 10:40-42
1 Timothy 5:8
Hebrews 13:2
3 John 1:7-8
2 John 1:7-11

Chapter 26
Hospitality

> *Definition: The special ability to address the physical and emotional needs of others in such a way that they feel comfortable and valued*

As a quality of God

God exemplified the perfect host in Genesis 2:15-18 by providing great hospitality to Adam. In the Garden of Eden, God gave Adam beautiful and comfortable surroundings and plentiful food to meet his physical needs and to please his senses. He gave Adam responsibilities to provide a sense of purpose and importance. To protect him from harm, God warned Adam about what he must avoid and told him the consequences of disobedience; at the same time, he offered Adam acceptable alternatives to the one thing that was to be denied him. He also provided for Adam's emotional needs by providing a suitable companion for him.

As illustrated in the Old Testament

Leviticus 19:33-34 specifies God's command to His people to treat outsiders in such a way that they felt valued and welcome.

Rahab demonstrated hospitality by protecting the spies who came to her house (Joshua 2:1-15), because she believed that their God would ultimately be victorious over the land. She requested that, when that time came, her kindness be reciprocated. Although she had an ulterior motive for her hospitality, she met the needs of the spies and provided for their safety and welfare despite great personal risk to herself.

Proverbs 25:21-22 admonishes us to extend hospitality toward all, providing for the physical requirements of food and water even for our enemies. This is echoed in Matthew 5:43-48, in which we are told to love our enemies and pray for those who persecute us. (This is not easy. Especially in light of the warning given in 2 John 1:7-11, regarding deceivers and the spirit of the antichrist, we must rely on the Holy Spirit to give us discernment and instruct us when it is or is not suitable—and to what degree—to extend hospitality to our enemies.)

As exemplified in Jesus' ministry

Besides addressing the spiritual needs of His audience, Jesus provided for the physical needs of the crowds that had come to hear him teach (John 8:13-21; John 15:32-38). He also used the opportunity to address the emotional needs of His disciples by assuring them that He could satisfy any hunger, affirming with the remaining seven basketfuls that He would supply not only sufficiently but generously.

As illustrated in the New Testament

Jesus taught, in Luke 10:38-42, that making a person feel welcome is more important than all the preparations related to impressing guests. It's easy to get so caught up in the *doing* that we lose sight of *who* we're doing it for and *why* we're doing it in the first place.

Barnabas practiced hospitality by welcoming Saul in Acts 9:26-28, introducing him to the apostles as a believer, opening social doors for him, and otherwise addressing Saul's needs to make him feel accepted in the Christian community. Extending hospitality to others doesn't necessarily require taking in house guests. We can be hospitable in any setting by welcoming others and addressing their physical and emotional needs as the Holy Spirit directs us.

Related teachings

Jesus reminded His disciples in Matthew 10:11-15 that, as guests, we have the responsibility of being considerate and bringing peace and blessing to the household we visit.

Also, just as we are expected to be hospitable to others of good will, we should expect to be treated hospitably. We are warned to have nothing to do with those who make us unwelcome or who make our mission more difficult (Matthew 10:11-14).

Yet, we should not be overly demanding. Note Jesus' reassurance to Martha in Luke 10:40-42 that really very little was required to make Him feel welcome. Instilling a sense of personal value was far more important than making elaborate preparations.

According to 1Timothy 5:8, God expects all of us to be hospitable to our families, providing for their physical and emotional well-being. He holds us responsible for that, so hospitality to that extent probably does not require any special gifting.

We are reminded in Hebrews 13:2 to be hospitable to those outside the family as well—even to strangers. Whether they are human or angelic, we don't know what purposes God might have in bringing them into our field of influence and care or what blessings He may want to bestow upon us through them.

Showing hospitality to those who work for the sake of Christ assists them in their work efforts (3 John 1:7-8).

However, as we have seen, offering hospitality to known deceivers is an entirely different matter. We are warned in 2 John 1:7-11 against taking deceivers and those acting in the spirit of the antichrist into our homes; offering them our hospitality indicates that we are providing them our protection, assisting them in their efforts, and in effect, aiding and abetting the enemy, even sharing in their deceptions. Because our apparent show of support lends them credence, others who trust us may be more trusting of them, as well. We must rely on the Holy Spirit to provide discernment and clearly reveal His will to us when we are in doubt.

Chapter 27

MERCY

---

*Definition: The special ability to translate
the desire to ease another's burden
into action to successfully do so*

Scriptures cited in Chapter 27 – Mercy

As a quality of God
Genesis 2:18
Psalm 72:12-14

As illustrated in the Old Testament
Job 29:11-17
Ruth 3:7-15
Jeremiah 38:4-13

As exemplified in Jesus' ministry
Matthew 9:36
Matthew 14:14
Mark 1:41
Matthew 9:24
John 11:17-44
Matthew 15:32

As illustrated in the New Testament
Acts 7:60
Acts 16:27-34

Related teachings
Proverbs 3:27-28
1John 17-18
James 2:12-17
Matthew. 5:7
Psalm 41:1-3
Romans 5:6-8

Chapter 27
Mercy

Definition: The special ability to translate the desire to ease another's burden into action to successfully do so

As a quality of God

From the very beginning of mankind, God has set us an example of mercy. Because He recognized the need in Adam for companionship of his own kind, He devised a way to meet that need. He provided Eve as a suitable companion and helper for Adam (Genesis 2:18). We see mercy in the very nature of God in Psalm 72:12-14: "For he will deliver the needy who cry out, the afflicted who have no one to help. He will take pity on the weak and the needy and save the needy from death. He will rescue them from oppression and violence, for precious is their blood in his sight."

As illustrated in the Old Testament

God also expects His people, who were created in His image, to show mercy to others, as illustrated in Job 29:11-17. In this passage, Job was commended because he rescued the poor who cried for help and helped those who had no other protector. He made their approaching death easier for the dying, and lifted the hearts of the bereaved. He was righteous and just. He helped the blind and the lame. He did whatever he could to make life easier for others and to help where help was needed.

In Ruth 3:7-15, Boaz recognized Ruth's need for a kinsman redeemer and agreed to provide for her, first by presenting her need to a nearer kinsman redeemer who had first claim, and, if that approach proved unsuccessful, to act as her kinsman redeemer himself, as she had requested. In the meantime, he provided her with what protection and provision he could to ease her physical, emotional, psychological, and financial needs.

Ebed-Melech the Cushite showed mercy when he drew the condemned prophet Jeremiah out of the cistern where he had been imprisoned, even providing padding to protect him from the ropes with which he was hoisted (Jeremiah 38:4-13). Our mercy is an expression and extension of God's love. The people around Jeremiah despised him, but he was a man on God's mission, and God provided for him through the mercy of Ebed-Melech.

As exemplified in Jesus' ministry

Jesus expressed mercy throughout His earthly ministry as He "had compassion" (Matthew 9:36) and met the needs of those around Him by healing diseases (Matthew 14:14; Mark 1:41), restoring physical and spiritual life (Matthew 9:24; John 11:17-44), and feeding those whom He continually encountered who expressed physical and spiritual hunger (Matthew 15:32).

As illustrated in the New Testament

The loving mercy that Jesus exhibited by dying on the cross as a sacrifice for all people was soon expressed also by Stephen. Even in the midst of being stoned, Stephen used his energy to cry out not for mercy for himself but for mercy on those who were in the very act of killing him (Acts 7:60).

In a similar way, Paul and Silas took time to show mercy and love to their jailer when the way was open for their escape from prison. Their concern and self-sacrifice resulted in the opportunity to witness to the jailer and to his entire family, who, in turn, showed mercy to them by washing their wounds and providing them dinner (Acts 16:27-34).

Related teachings

Mercy is timely; it doesn't wait on our convenience. Proverbs 3:27-28 instructs us to not withhold good from those who deserve it when it is in our power to act. Don't tell someone to "come back tomorrow" if you can provide for their needs immediately.

The Apostle John taught that we are to love not merely with words but with actions; we are to use our material possessions to express our concern for those in need (1 John 17-18).

In James 2:12-17, James repeatedly presses his point that our expressions of mercy will be judged. If we judge others without mercy, God will judge us in the same way. Without activity that backs up what we profess, our "faith" is meaningless and without value; in the same way, without action to back it up, mercy is non-existent. Yet if we express mercy in our dealings with others, God will be merciful to us (Matthew 5:7; Psalm 41:1-3).

God showed us mercy when He saved us from our sins (Romans 5:6-8) while we were still in bondage to those sins. In the same way, He expects us to show mercy to others, even while they are undeserving. It is not in the nature of man to show such mercy; it is in the nature of God. We can be merciful to this greater extent only by the power of God's Holy Spirit acting through us.

Chapter 28

INTERCESSION

Definition: The special ability to present specific needs of other people to God on their behalf

---

Scriptures cited in Chapter 28 – Intercession

As a quality of God
John 17:6-9
Romans 8:26-27
Matthew 5:44-48
John 3:16

As illustrated in the Old Testament
Job 16:19-21
Hebrews 7:25
Numbers 11:1-2
Numbers 16:46-48
1 Samuel 7:5-6
Samuel 12:23
2 Samuel 24:25
Job 42:8-9
Psalm 122:6-9
2 Chronicles 7:14
Ezekiel 22:30

As exemplified in Jesus' ministry
Hebrews 7:25
Matthew 14:23
Matthew 6:5-15
Matthew 19:13-15
Matthew 5:44
Luke 6:27-29
Luke 23:33-34
Luke 22:32
John 17:9-18:1

As illustrated in the New Testament
Acts 14:23
Galatians 6:2
James 5:15-16
Jude 1:20
Romans 8:26-27

Related teachings
Luke 11:9
Luke 18:1
Luke 18:7
Mark 11:24
Ephesians 6:18-20
Matthew 18:19-20
Matthew 26:36-41
Luke 18:9-14
1 Timothy 2:1-4
1 John 5:14-15

Intercessory Suggestions:
Ephesians 1:16-19
Ephesians 3:12-19
Ephesians 6:18-20
Colossians 1:9-12
Colossians 4:2-4
Colossians 4:12
2 Thessalonians 1:11-12
2 Thessalonians 3:1-3
1 Timothy 2:1-4
Philemon 1:6

Chapter 28

Intercession

Definition: The special ability to present specific needs of other people to God on their behalf

As a quality of God

God is holy, separated from all unrighteousness—from anything that is wrong or sinful. As humans, descended from the disobedient Adam, we are born with a sin nature. So we cannot go directly before God in our sinful state. Yet the Father provides intercessors for us to bridge the gap between us and Himself.

His Son, Jesus, though also holy, humbled Himself to live among us, and has thereby experienced the same temptations that we experience. Being without sin, Jesus can go into the Father's presence to plead with Him; and, having experienced the trials of life in a physical, human body, Jesus can identify with us as our brother. Jesus, therefore, is a fully qualified intermediary between the Father and those of us in the earthly realm whom God has called to faith in Him (John 17:6-9).

The Holy Spirit, the very essence of God's nature, intercedes for us as well, searching our hearts and interceding according to God's will when we don't know what to pray, to help us in our weakness (Romans 8:26-27).

Jesus calls those who intercede for their enemies "sons of your Father in heaven" (Matthew 5:44-48) because intercession is an expression of perfect, Godly love. The Father's perfect love blesses the unjust as well as the just, the undeserving as much as the deserving. It is that love and grace—that overriding aspect of God's nature—that provides for intercession (John 3:16).

As illustrated in the Old Testament

Job acknowledged his faith in a God-provided intercessor (Job 16:19-21). Although Job had no name for Him at that time, we now know Him to be Jesus, our advocate in heaven, interceding on behalf of all those who put their faith in Christ (Hebrews 7:25).

Throughout the Old Testament, God called for intercession. Moses interceded for the Israelites who complained on their journey to the Promised Land (Numbers 11:1-2), and he directed Aaron to make atonement for them (Numbers 16:46-48). Samuel recognized his responsibility to pray and intercede with God for the people entrusted to his care (1 Samuel 7:5-6; Samuel 12:23). These intercessors were called by God to bear responsibility for the people, so they were empowered by the Holy Spirit to serve in an intercessory capacity. Because Christ had not yet provided the sacrifice to atone for all sin, intercession in the Old Testament was often combined with sacrifice and atonement for sin, as it was when King David sought relief for his people who were suffering because of his personal sin (2 Samuel 24:25).

Even though Job, who trusted in a heavenly advocate, was to intercede for his friends, they were told to sacrifice because of their own foolishness (Job 42:8-9). Job's faith in God's grace through the coming Christ opened God's ears to him, but his friends needed to express their repentance through sacrifice.

The psalmist sang to "pray for the peace of Jerusalem," seeking its wellbeing and asking for peace within its walls (Psalm 122:6-9). God demanded conditions for such intercession. He told Solomon, "if my people, who are called by my name, will humble themselves and pray and seek my face and turn from their wicked ways, then will I hear from heaven and will forgive their sin and will heal their land" (2 Chronicles 7:14). Intercession requires humility, a true desire for contact with God, and repentance from sin.

God spoke to the prophet Ezekiel, expressing sorrow that no one was willing to "build up the wall and stand before me in the gap on behalf of the land so I would not have to destroy it" (Ezekiel 22:30). The wall was a literal, physical entity that had been destroyed and needed to be rebuilt to protect the inhabitants of the city. We can extrapolate from that, however, that it also represents a spiritual wall that protects God's people. That wall can be breached by the enemy and will continue to deteriorate, due to ambivalence and neglect, unless the body of believers steps forward to rebuild it and intercede for those at risk. God wants us to care enough to intercede for our nation, for the Church body, and for our neighbors.

As exemplified in Jesus' ministry

Hebrews 7:25 tells us that Jesus lives to intercede for those who draw near to God through Him.

We are told in Matthew 14:23 that Jesus went off by Himself to pray. Prayer is a very personal communication between mankind and God. Although prayer can be raised in concert, as in corporate prayer, when many people pray simultaneously for the same thing, it is primarily a private conversation and should never be for show (Matthew 6:5-15).

Intercession and blessing should not be limited by age or understanding (Matthew 19:13-15).

Jesus taught in Matthew 5:44 and again in Luke 6:27-29 to "love your enemies, do good to those who hate you, bless those who curse you, pray for those who mistreat you." He exhibited that grace Himself on the cross, when He prayed for those who mocked and tortured Him (Luke 23:33-34).

He prayed for Peter that his faith would not fail (Luke 22:32); and that he could then strengthen the other apostles. Jesus also prayed for the other disciples (John 17:9-18:1) and for all who would follow in subsequent generations of believers.

As illustrated in the New Testament

The apostles in Acts 14:23 selected elders and commended them to God through prayer. Prayer is often accompanied by fasting as a means of humbling the soul before God.

Paul encourages us in Galatians 6:2 to carry one another's burdens, which includes interceding for one another's needs. James, too, (James 5:15-16) encourages us to confess our sins to one another and pray for each other. Acknowledging our sins keeps us humble and sympathetic toward one another, more ready to enter into prayer on others' behalf.

And perhaps most importantly of all, Jude 1:20 tells us to pray in the Holy Spirit, Who intercedes for us, according to the will of God, "with groans that words cannot express" (Romans 8:26-27).

Related teachings

Jesus taught that we are to be persistent in our requests (Luke 11:9; Luke 18:1; Luke 18:7): to ask and keep asking, pray and don't lose heart; and to cry out to Him day and night.

He told us in Mark 11:24 that whatever we pray and ask, if we believe we have received the petition it will be granted.

We are told in Ephesians 6:18-20 to pray in the Spirit and to pray specifically for the leaders and teachers of the gospel that they may teach accurately and fearlessly, and that the Lord will provide the words to speak.

Corporate prayer is powerful when we agree in accord with Christ (Matthew 18:19-20).

Matthew 26:36-41 suggests that, as Jesus sought the companionship of His disciples in the Garden of Gethsemane, the presence and prayerful support of others is comforting when one is troubled and seeking God's presence. There we can intercede with humility for one another's needs (Luke 18:9-14).

1 Timothy 2:1-4 teaches us that requests, prayers, intercession, and thanksgiving should be made for everyone, including all those in authority. It is not only in times of spiritual decadence that we must pray for our national and international leaders. We should pray in good times and bad times, for individuals close to us and for those we don't know. We are called to pray for God's guiding hand on both moral leaders and corrupt leaders, whether they are of our political leanings

or not. This is spiritual warfare. If we don't pray that our leaders will have Godly counsel, how can we expect them to make Godly decisions? The responsibility of leadership does not fall on the shoulders of only one man or of one political party but of the entire nation.

"This is the confidence that we have in approaching God: that if we ask anything according to his will, he hears us. And if we know that he hears—whatever we ask—we know that we have what we asked of Him" (1 John 5:14-15).

Scriptural suggestions to pray on others' behalf

Ephesians 1:16-19

16 I have not stopped *giving thanks for you*, remembering you in my prayers.

17 *I keep asking that the God of our Lord Jesus Christ, the glorious Father, may give you the Spirit of wisdom and revelation, so that you may know him better.*

18 *I pray also that the eyes of your heart may be enlightened in order that you may know the hope to which he has called you, the riches of his glorious inheritance in the saints,*

19 *and his incomparably great power for us who believe.* That power is like the working of his mighty strength,

Ephesians 3:12-19

12 In him and through faith in him we may approach God with freedom and confidence.

13 I ask you, therefore, *not to be discouraged* because of my sufferings for you, which are your glory.

14 For this reason I kneel before the Father,

15 from whom his whole family in heaven and on earth derives its name.

16 I pray that *out of his glorious riches he may strengthen you with power through his Spirit in your inner being,*

17 *so that Christ may dwell in your hearts through faith. And I pray that you, being rooted and established in love,*

18 *may have power, together with all the saints, to grasp how wide and long and high and deep is the love of Christ,*

19 *and to know this love that surpasses knowledge—that you may be filled to the measure of all the fullness of God.*

Ephesians 6:18-20

18 And *pray in the Spirit on all occasions with all kinds of prayers and requests.* With this in mind, *be alert and always keep on praying for all the saints.*

19 *Pray also for me, that whenever I open my mouth, words may be given me so that I will fearlessly make known the mystery of the gospel,*

20 for which I am an ambassador in chains. *Pray that I may declare it fearlessly, as I should.*

Colossians 1:9-12

9 For this reason, since the day we heard about you, we have not stopped praying for you and *asking God to fill you with the knowledge of his will through all spiritual wisdom and understanding.*

10 *And we pray this in order that you may live a life worthy of the Lord and may please him in every way: bearing fruit in every good work, growing in the knowledge of God,*

11 *being strengthened with all power according to his glorious might so that you may have great endurance and patience, and joyfully*

12 *giving thanks to the Father,* who has qualified you to share in the inheritance of the saints in the kingdom of light.

Colossians 4:2-4

2 *Devote yourselves to prayer, being watchful and thankful.*

3 *And pray for us, too, that God may open a door for our message, so that we may proclaim the mystery of Christ,* for which I am in chains.

4 *Pray that I may proclaim it clearly, as I should.*

Colossians 4:12

12 Epaphras … is always wrestling in prayer for you, *that you may stand firm in all the will of God, mature and fully assured.*

2 Thessalonians 1:11-12

11 With this in mind, *we constantly pray for you, that our God may count you worthy of his calling, and that by his power he may fulfill every good purpose of yours and every act prompted by your faith.*

12 *We pray this so that the name of our Lord Jesus may be glorified in you, and you in him, according to the grace of our God and the Lord Jesus Christ.*

2 Thessalonians 3:1-3

1 Finally, brothers, *pray for us that the message of the Lord may spread rapidly and be honored, just as it was with you.*

2 *And pray that we may be delivered from wicked and evil men, for not everyone has faith.*

3 *But the Lord is faithful, and he will strengthen and protect you from the evil one.*

1 Timothy 2:1-4

1 I urge, then, first of all, that *requests, prayers, intercession and thanksgiving be made for everyone*

2 *for kings and all those in authority, that we may live peaceful and quiet lives in all godliness and holiness.*

3 This is good, and pleases God our Savior,

4 *who wants all men to be saved and to come to a knowledge of the truth.*

Philemon 1:6

6 *I pray that you may be active in sharing your faith, so that you will have a full understanding of every good thing we have in Christ.*

Chapter 29

DRIVING OUT SPIRITS

Definition: The special ability to expel spirits from a stronghold by the power of the Holy Spirit

---

Scriptures cited in Chapter 29 – Driving Out Spirits

As a quality of God
Deuteronomy 5:6-10
Psalm 18:43-45

As illustrated in the Old Testament
Psalm 44:2-7
Psalm 118:10-12
1 Samuel 16:14-23
1 Samuel 16:14
1 Samuel 16:23

As exemplified in Jesus' ministry
1 John 3:8
Luke 4:33-36, 41
Luke 8:27-33
Matthew 8:28-34
Psalm 18:43-45
Mark 16:9
Luke 8:2
Luke 10:17-22

As illustrated in the New Testament
Luke 10:17-19
Acts 5:16
Acts 19:13-20

Related teachings
Matthew 10:1-8
1 Samuel 16:23
Matthew 12:22
Matthew 8:28-34
Luke 4:33-34
Acts 16:17-18
2 Peter 3:9

John 8:44
2 Timothy 1:7
Revelation 12:10
1 Corinthians 14:33
Leviticus 19:31
1 Samuel 30:3-6
Leviticus 19:31
2 Corinthians 11:14
Acts 16:16-18
Ephesians 4:27
James 2:19
Acts 19:13-20
Luke 9:49-50
Mark 9:38
Luke 9:49-50
Ephesians 6:10-18
Acts 21:31-32

Driving Out Spirits

> *Definition: The special ability to expel spirits from a stronghold by the power of the Holy Spirit*

As a quality of God

God loves and protects those who follow Him, but he opposes those who work against him (Deuteronomy 5:6-10). He refers to Himself as a jealous God. (Note that this is quite different from "envy," with which "jealousy" is often confused. Envy or covetousness is the desire for something that belongs to another, whereas jealousy is being protective of that which is one's own.)

In Psalm 18:43-45, we see a likeness or "type" of Christ in the psalmist David; the "people I did not know" and "foreigners" may be interpreted as non-believers and demons—those formerly under the regime of another ruler. The psalmist recognizes that it is God the Father who provides deliverance from all the opposing forces.

As illustrated in the Old Testament

The psalmist of Psalm 44:2-7 recognized that it was God who had protected the land and people, that their own military strength alone would not have been sufficient. Likewise, Psalm 118:10-12 acknowledges that it was only the Lord's supporting strength and protection that had achieved the victory in what would have been a lost cause without it.

When the Spirit of the Lord departed from Saul, an "evil spirit from God" took its place (1 Samuel 16:14-23). It is unclear whether this evil spirit was sent directly from God or whether it was actually demonic in origin but was used by God to establish David as an influential member of Saul's household. Saul had rejected God, turning to the occult for answers, thereby opening the door for God to permit demonic activity to affect him (v. 14). In 1 Samuel 16:23, we see David ministering to

Saul and providing relief through music. If this was indeed a form of "casting out demons," the result each time appears to have had only a temporary effect because Saul's heart had not been changed.

As exemplified in Jesus' ministry

According to 1 John 3:8, Jesus' primary purpose for His coming to earth was to destroy the works of the devil. We are given numerous examples of His driving out demons and evil spirits.

Luke 4:33-36 and 4:41 illustrate the power of Jesus over demonic spirits. The demons themselves recognized that Jesus was the Son of God. Although they spoke the truth of Who He was, they were not speaking in accordance with His will. He rebuked them for announcing Who He was because He was not yet ready to reveal Himself as the Christ. They had no choice but to obey Him.

When confronted by the demon-possessed man in Luke 8:27-33, Jesus was able to treat the demonic spirit as an individual apart from the man, to whom He extended mercy. He commanded that the evil spirits (who were, by their own admission, multiple) to separate themselves from the human body they were controlling. These spirits, too, had no option but to comply with Jesus' command.

A similar account is given in Matthew 8:28-34, in which two demon-possessed men confronted Jesus. In this case, too, Jesus commanded the demonic spirits to leave the men. At the spirits' request, He sent them into a nearby herd of pigs, which stampeded away from His presence to their demise. The whole town became fearful of Jesus because of the power He demonstrated and, like the demonic spirits had before them, wanted Him to stay far away from them. Note the similarity of response between this and the foreigners of Psalm 18:43-45.

Although we don't directly see the event described in the scriptures, we are told twice that Jesus had cast out seven demons from Mary Magdalen (Mark 16:9; Luke 8:2).

Jesus acknowledged in Luke 10:17-22 that He had seen a vision of the results of the disciples' successful efforts in casting out demonic spirits. However, He reminded them, they should not rejoice in their own abilities but acknowledge that their success was only by the power of God working to extend mercy to others, just as God had previously extended it to them. In the same way that He taught His disciples not to rejoice on their own account that the spirits submitted to them but that they should rejoice in the Father's work on their behalf, Jesus acknowledged the Father's hand in the work He did, thanking the Father for the unexpected way in which it had pleased God to accomplish it.

As illustrated in the New Testament

The Gospel of Luke tells us that when Jesus had sent seventy-two followers out in pairs to minister, they returned joyfully with news that "even the demons submit to us in your name" (Luke 10:17-19). He confirmed their success by telling them, "I saw Satan fall like lightning from heaven. I have given you authority to trample on snakes and scorpions and to overcome all the power of the enemy; nothing will harm you."

The writer of the Acts of the Apostles tells us that "Crowds gathered also from the towns around Jerusalem, bringing their sick and those tormented by evil spirits, and all of them were healed" (Acts 5:16).

But not all those attempting to exorcize demons were believers in Christ. Acts 19:13-20 records that although the spirits recognized the names of both Jesus and those whom He had authorized, the demons did not recognize those who took Jesus's name in vain, merely using it as a kind of magical incantation rather than as a sincere appeal for the Lord's help through the power of the Holy Spirit.

Related teachings

When Jesus sent out His twelve disciples (Matthew 10:1-8), He told them to drive out evil spirits and gave them the authority to do so.

In the context of today's society in the United States, most of us don't normally think of demonic spirits as being an evident problem. It might be more accurate to say that we have come to accept the activity of demonic spirits as so normal that we don't recognize its source. Yet, when we compare our lives with those we find chronicled in the Old Testament, we find many similarities. In 1 Samuel 16:23, Saul, from whom God's Spirit had departed, was tormented by evil spirits, much as many people today are. Today such people are hospitalized, counseled, or medicated. For Saul, relief was found only through the musical ministrations of David, who was anointed by God.

Demon-possession can appear in other forms, as well. In Matthew 12:22, a demon-possessed man who was blind and mute was brought to Jesus. When Jesus cast out the demon, the man became able to both see and speak.

Many of our homeless today are suffering from psychiatric and social handicaps. They probably aren't so very different from the demoniacs Jesus encountered in the region of the Gadarenes in Matthew 8:28-34, who lived in the tombs, away from the rest of society, and were so violent that people were afraid to approach them.

And how often today do we hear people mocking God, or mocking others' faith in Christ, as the demoniac in Luke 4:33-34, or the fortune teller in Acts 16:17-18, may have been doing?

But though God is patient with us and wants everyone to find their salvation in Him (2 Peter 3:9), Satan's purpose is to separate us from God. Satan makes his inroads through deception (John 8:44), fear (2 Timothy 1:7), accusations (Revelation 12:10), and confusion (1 Corinthians 14:33).

There is still a need to drive out the spirit of Satan that lives among us. Yet we must heed God's warning not to turn to mediums or seek out spiritists (Leviticus 19:31). We are instead to turn to God for the information and the solutions needed. Just as David and his men, who discovered that their wives and children had been taken captive from Ziklag (1 Samuel 30:3-6), we may discover to our extreme grief that our loved ones have been taken captive by the enemy of our souls, through deception, fear, accusations (including hatred, unforgiveness, and suspicion), and confusion (such as doubt or distractions). Then, when those around us turn against us and our faith because of those same circumstances, as David's men threatened to turn against him, we, like David, can find strength and answers in the Lord.

Even today we may see television ads for clairvoyants; newspapers featuring "entertainment" horoscopes; and window signs calling attention to palm-readers and other forms of fortune-telling. These are the very "mediums" we are warned against in Leviticus 19:31 and again in 2 Corinthians 11:14. People who practice or seek information from occult methods of foretelling the future open themselves to demonic activity and deception, even though what they learn may appear to be true, as we hear in the cries of the slave girl's spirit of divination in Acts 16:16-18. By applying to them (even "just for fun") we leave ourselves open to such activity and deception as well. Even fortune-telling games and pastimes can tantalize and lure us away from our reliance on God's providence. Instead we are told to resist the devil (and his temptations) and he will flee from us (Ephesians 4:27).

The demons know who belongs to Christ and whom they must obey (James 2:19). They also know who is not of Christ. Counterfeit works, attempted for the wrong reasons, as depicted in Acts 19:13-20, are not effective for God's purposes. However, Jesus is glorified through the effective work of His people. We do not always know who may be doing the Lord's work. Therefore, according to the Apostle John's teachings in Luke 9:49-50, if the purpose is within God's will, and if it is apparently effective toward that end, we should not interfere. We are not to deter others who cast out spirits in the name of Christ (Mark 9:38; Luke 9:49-50).

Whereas believers in the Old Testament usually tried to achieve their victories against the enemy militarily, Jesus taught His followers to seek a spiritual victory over the enemy. Both forms of warfare demand full reliance on and recognition of the need for God's help. Ephesians 6:10-18 reminds us that we must remain alert to who our opponent is, apply the protections God has provided for us, and always be prepared for battle against "the spiritual forces of evil in the heavenly realms."

A physical illustration of spiritual warfare can be observed in Acts 21:31-32. Paul was under attack by the citizens of Jerusalem. The commander of the Roman troops (who, in this instance, is a "type" or representation of Christ, the head of the Church) enlisted assistance from both officers and soldiers (who represent angels and Paul's fellow believers, respectively) to go to the aid of Paul, who was a Roman citizen (representing a citizen of the Kingdom of God) and hence under the protection of the Roman jurisdiction (representative, in this case, of God's Kingdom). When the rioters (the embodiment here of demonic spirits) saw the approaching troops, they abandoned their attack on Paul.

Chapter 30

HEALINGS

Definition: The special ability to effect healing for an individual, by the power of the Holy Spirit, from diseases and impairments without relying on medical intervention

---

Scriptures cited in Chapter 30 – Healings

As a quality of God
Exodus 15:22-26
Numbers 21:9
Deuteronomy 32:39
Deuteronomy 28:58-60
Deuteronomy 29:22
Psalm 103:3-4
Psalm 146:8
Psalm 147:3

As illustrated in the Old Testament
Exodus 32:4
Numbers 21:9
2 Samuel 12:13-23
1 Kings 17:17-24
2 Kings 5:11, 14

As exemplified in Jesus' ministry
Matthew 14:35-36
Matthew 20:34
Matthew 21:14
Mark 7:32-35
Mark 5:25-34
Matthew 8:4
Matthew 9:6
Mark 2:10-12
Mark 3:1-5
Mark 5:19, 35-42
Mark 7:32-35
John 4:50
John 5:8
Luke 4:38-40
Mark 8:22-25
Luke 5:12-13
Luke 5:15-17
John 5:30

John 8:28-29
John 14:10-21
Luke 5:18-25
Luke 7:2-10
John 5:3-14

As illustrated in the New Testament
Acts 3:2-10
Acts 3:2-16
Acts 5:12-16
Acts 9:17-19
Acts 9:32-35
Acts 14:8-10
Acts 28:8-9
Acts 14:11-18

Related teachings
2 Corinthians 12:7-10
James 5:14-16
Psalm 107:17-20
Psalm 107:21-22
Isaiah 53:4
Matthew 10:8
2 Chronicles 32:24-25
2 Corinthians 12:9-10

Healings

> *Definition: The special ability to effect healing for an individual, by the power of the Holy Spirit, from diseases and impairments without relying on medical intervention*

As a quality of God

Just as God sweetened the bitter waters of Marah during the Exodus from Egypt (Exodus 15:22-26) and provided the bronze serpent as a focal point for those who would seek His healing from the venomous snake bites (Numbers 21:9), He promised to be their healer if the people heeded God and His commandments.

In Deuteronomy 32:39, He reminded them that it is He who ultimately decides between life and death—death for those who disobey and turn away from Him (Deuteronomy 28:58-60) and for serving other gods (Deuteronomy 29:22); healing and life for those who repent (Psalm 103:3-4).

God heals both physical ailments (Psalm 146:8) and emotional distress (Psalm 147:3).

As illustrated in the Old Testament

In the Old Testament, it appears that God permitted disease for several reasons, among them, disobedience or unfaithfulness to Him or as a consequence of sin. In Job's case, it was a test of Job's faithfulness. In each case, God's purpose is to instill in His people an understanding of His supremacy and ultimately draw them into closer relationship with Him.

God provided Moses a tangible symbol to which the people could turn to remind them of both their sin and His healing power. Unlike the golden calf (Exodus 32:4), the bronze serpent of Numbers 21:9 was not to be treated as an idol but instead was used to remind the people of the presence of the living God.

Sometimes God's answer to our prayers for healing is "no," as it was when David prayed that Bathsheba's child would survive (2 Samuel 12:13-23). Even forgiven sin has consequences and, like David, we must be ready to accept God's judgment and move on. Other times, God heals and restores as confirmation of the message of His saving grace and to affirm the veracity of His servants, as He did in 1 Kings 17:17-24.

Healings need not come through showy displays, as Naaman expected in 2 Kings 5:11, but by obedience and faith (2 Kings 5:14).

As exemplified in Jesus' ministry

In contrast with the Old Testament, the emphasis in the New Testament is not on disease but on healing—overcoming disease and disability by the power of the Holy Spirit, through the mercy and grace of Christ Jesus.

Throughout the Gospels, Jesus appears to have responded positively to those who came to him for healing (Matthew 14:35-36); He restored sight to the blind (Matthew 20:34). He healed the lame (Matthew 21:14). He opened the ears of the deaf (Mark 7:32-35). It was not His physical touch but their faith in Him that healed them (Mark 5:25-34). Notice that in many cases, His healing involved an action or directive for (usually) the patient to act on as an indication of his faith or as a confirmation of Christ's authority to heal and to forgive sins (Matthew 8:4; Matthew 9:6; Mark 2:10-12; Mark 3:1-5; Mark 5:19,35-42; Mark 7:32-35; John 4:50; John 5:8).

Some healings appear to have been instantaneous, like that found in Luke 4:38-40; others occurred in stages (Mark 8:22-25).

In Luke 5:12-13 a leper approached Jesus with faith that Jesus was *able* to heal, and with humility, not demanding a healing, but leaving the decision up to the Lord.

The comment found in Luke 5:15-17, that "the power of the Lord was present for him to heal the sick" would seem to indicate that such power was not always present. He acted only in accordance with His Father's will (John 5:30; John 8:28-29; John 14:10-21). If Jesus submitted to God's will and recognized that there were times to use His healing power and times to refrain, we must recognize that as well.

On occasion, Jesus used healing as a sign and confirmation of greater grace, as he did in Luke 5:18-25. Jesus made it clear in Luke 7:2-10 that he was responding to the great faith the centurion expressed in seeking healing for his servant, even from a long distance.

We have much to learn from John 5:3-14. Please notice several things about this passage. The sick man had faith for healing—even if it was by another method. He had the desire to be healed, though the mat probably represented his livelihood and dependency as a beggar. He was obedient. Note that it was *that* man who was healed, not one of the others who also waited by the pool. He had been freed of his dependence on his mat; yet just as Satan tries to convince us we are still subject to the law, the Jews tried to tell him that he could not accept his healing by carrying his own mat and thereby leaving his "sickroom." When Jesus saw him again, He offered a warning, implying a purpose for the healing—to bring about repentance ("stop sinning or...") It was not a threat, but a reminder to make the best of the situation—to be healed of sins as well as of his physical disability, so that Satan would have no opportunity to entrap him again.

As illustrated in the New Testament

Healing, as shown in Acts 3:2-10, was used as evidence of the truth of the gospel message, introducing others to the availability of salvation through Christ. The crippled man whose story is told in Acts 3:2-16 did not seek healing but was encouraged to believe it was possible. His healing was used as an encouragement to others.

Again, in Acts 5:12-16, the message of Christ's healing grace was spread widely as "the apostles performed many miraculous signs and wonders among the people. ... and all of them were healed."

Despite all earthly evidence that he should be wary, Ananias (Acts

9:17-19) trusted God when called to approach Saul of Tarsus with the message of Christ's healing and grace. "Immediately ... he could see again." Saul's healing occurred in conjunction with his baptism and infilling of the Holy Spirit.

Acts 9:32-35, Acts 14:8-10, and Acts 28:8-9 illustrate additional situations in which healings served to draw people to the Lord. The Apostle Paul also used the gift of discernment to recognize that the lame man had faith to be healed. He used the opportunity in Acts 14:11-18 to correct mistaken assumptions and to preach the good news of the living God.

Related teachings

Although Paul obviously had faith for healing and had the gift of healing others, the Lord had a reason to say "no" to his prayers for his own deliverance (2 Corinthians 12:7-10). Paul's ministry was stronger, due to his afflictions, because Christ's power was in greater evidence when contrasted with Paul's weakness.

It is not only the faith of the sick person that decides the efficacy of a prayer for healing. James 5:14-16 tells us that the one who prays must also have faith for the healing. We must confess our own sins, be cleansed, and pray for one another. Only when we seek God's will can our prayers be fully effective.

Psalm 107:17-20 tells us that despite afflictions brought on by our rebellious ways, God still hears our cries of distress and provides the healing we need. In response (Psalm 107:21-22), we are to give thanks to the Lord and tell others of His works on our behalf.

According to Isaiah 53:4, Christ has borne the punishment in our place for the sins we commit. And the wounds He suffered were so that our healing can take place. In response, we are to reciprocate by playing it forward: "Freely you have received, freely give" (Matthew 10:8), as the Holy Spirit empowers us. This is His directive to us as believers and disciples.

Those who receive healings should reciprocate through humility and obedience. Notice that, as related in 2 Chronicles 32:24-25, King Hezekiah returned no benefit for the healing and sign he had received, resulting in God's wrath on him and on the nation.

Healings and repentance don't always go hand-in-hand. But healings may be used to illustrate forgiveness or God's power and grace. They are granted for God's purposes. He chooses when and how to effect healing. As Paul pointed out in 2 Corinthians 12:9-10, ultimately, the Lord's response to our prayers for healing is to serve His purpose of strengthening the Church.

Chapter 31

RESURRECTIONS

Definition: The special ability, by the power of the Holy Spirit, to restore to life, without the help of medical or mechanical means, one who has died

---

Scriptures cited in Chapter 31 – Resurrections

As a quality of God
Genesis 1:20-27
Genesis 2:15-17
Genesis 3:1-19
1 John 3:8
Romans 4:25
Romans 5:12-19
Ezekiel 18:32
Psalm 116:15

As illustrated in the Old Testament
1 Kings 17:8-24
2 Kings 4:8-37
2 Kings 13:20-21
1 Peter 4:6

As exemplified in Jesus' ministry
John 5:21
Mark 5:22-24
Mark 5:25-34
Mark 5:35-41
Luke 7:12-16
John 11:1-15
John 11:8
John 11:38-45
Matthew 17:22-23
Luke 24:20-24
Matthew 28:1-10
John 20:1-29
Matthew 27:63-66
John 21:1-24
Mark 16:19
Luke 24:50-51

As illustrated in the New Testament
Acts 2:1-4
Acts 9:36-4
Acts 20:9-12

Related teachings
Acts 26:8
Ezekiel 18:32
Genesis 5:24
2 Kings 2:11-12
Hebrews 11:5-6
1 Thessalonians 4:16-17
1 Corinthians 15:20-24
1 Corinthians 15:51-55

Chapter 31

Resurrections

> *Definition: The special ability, by the power of the Holy Spirit, to restore to life, without the help of medical or mechanical means, one who has died*

As a quality of God

The very nature of God is to provide life, as He did in the beginning when He created plants, animals, and mankind (Genesis 1:20-27). It was Satan, not God, who introduced death (Genesis 2:15-17; 3:1-19). It is God who provided the means for us to overcome death; He provided our substitute, in the person of Christ, to suffer the consequences of our sin, overcome the influence of Satan on our behalf (1 John 3:8), and provide us with a means to reclaim the life in God that we had lost through our sin-prone nature (Romans 4:25; 5:12-19).

God takes no pleasure in the death of anyone (Ezekiel 18:32). Psalm 116:15 says further that "Precious (important and no light matter) in the sight of the Lord is the death of His saints—His loving ones" (Amplified).

As illustrated in the Old Testament

God had provided for Elijah through the hospitality of the widow of Zarepath (1 Kings 17:8-24). He also provided for the widow's needs by continuously replenishing her supply of flour and oil. When her son's illness caused him to stop breathing, Elijah sought God's mercy on her again. He stretched himself over the child's body and prayed three times to the Lord before the boy returned to life. It was further confirmation to the widow that Elijah was indeed a man of God and that his prophecies were true.

The son of the Shunammite woman (2 Kings 4:8-37) had been a gift from God prophesied in appreciation of her hospitality to Elisha. Though in understandable distress at the child's death, she still expressed faith to her husband that "All will be well" (v. 23, NASB) and again to Elisha that "It is well" (v. 26, NASB). Elisha, like Elijah, sought the Lord's grace for her. He acted in faith that the Lord would respond, praying repeatedly until the boy returned to life.

Although in the preceding examples both Elijah and Elisha prayed multiple times before life was restored to the children, we read in 2 Kings 13:20-21 that after Elisha died and was entombed, the body of a dead man was unceremoniously thrust into Elisha's tomb and was instantly restored to life when it came into contact with Elisha's bones.

Having been dead for some time, the Prophet Elisha could not have sought restoration for the other dead man in the manner he had for the widow's son, so this event seems to indicate that Elisha's understanding and faith in God's resurrection power carried over even after his earthly death. If that is the case, it is also a strong indication of the continuation of Elisha's spiritual life subsequent to his earthly death (1 Peter 4:6).

As exemplified in Jesus' ministry

Jesus Himself tells us in John 5:21 that "Just as the Father raises the dead and gives them life, even so the Son also gives life to whom He wishes" (NASB).

A synagogue official had sought Jesus to ask Him to heal his daughter, who was dying (Mark 5:22-24). Even as Jesus approached the official's home He healed a woman in the crowd that pressed around Him (Mark 5:25-34). But before they reached the official's house, they received news of the girl's death (Mark 5:35-41). Jesus assured the official, "Don't be afraid; just believe." Jesus entered the room, took her hand, and told her to get up. She was immediately restored to life. Jesus honored the official's great faith in His ability to heal his daughter.

We read in Luke 7:12-16 that Jesus was moved by the plight of a widow whose son had died, much as Elijah had been. He showed mercy by restoring life to the dead man even as the mourners were carrying the body to the burial site. As a result, the people praised God.

When Jesus was notified that His friend Lazarus was sick, He deliberately delayed going to heal him, knowing that God had a greater purpose for the situation (John 11:1-15). He knew that the story would not end in Lazarus's death, despite strong evidence to the contrary. (Notice that Thomas, who speaks up in verse 16, couldn't see beyond the danger of returning to that area of Judea, as the disciples had pointed out in John 11:8.) In fact, Lazarus had been in the tomb for four days before Jesus went to him.

John 11:38-45 illustrates how Jesus took the opportunity to demonstrate His authority even over death. He wept (v. 35) not because Lazarus had died (see v. 4) but because the sisters were so distressed. Their faith, like Thomas's, was shaky and their understanding was incomplete. Through this delayed resurrection, He was illustrating for them His power over death. He used this opportunity to encourage and strengthen His followers in preparation for His own death and resurrection, reinforcing His assurance to Martha that "I am the resurrection and the life. He who believes in me will live, even though he dies; and whoever lives and believes in me will never die" (vv. 25-26).

Jesus had told His disciples of His own impending death and resurrection (Matthew 17:22-23). "The Son of Man is going to be betrayed into the hands of men. They will kill him, and on the third day He will be raised to life." This prophecy was carried out to the letter, as we are told in Luke 24:20-24. Although we aren't privy to the precise manner in which God resurrected His Son, Matthew 28:1-10 and John 20:1-29 provide a clear picture of the discovery of His resurrection. Not only was the tomb found empty, though it had been carefully and thoroughly sealed and guarded with armed soldiers (Matthew 27:63-66), but the resurrected Lord then appeared in the flesh and spoke to Mary Magdalene and on multiple occasions to the disciples as clear evidence (John 21:1-24) until He ascended into heaven (Mark 16:19; Luke 24:50-51).

As illustrated in the New Testament

Resurrections continued to occur in the New Testament Church following the Day of Pentecost, when so many believers were filled with the Holy Spirit (Acts 2:1-4). Peter raised Tabitha (Dorcas) from the dead (Acts 9:36-4). This not only restored one of Jesus' faithful servants to her useful position in the Church, easing the distress of many, but also served to draw in many new believers.

Again in Acts 20:9-12, we see Paul resurrect Eutychus. Whether it was Paul's remorse for putting one of his listeners to sleep, his mercy and compassion, or the Holy Spirit's directive that drove him downstairs to reclaim the young man's life in Jesus' name, God honored Paul's concern and faith to restore Eutychus to life.

Related teachings

"Why should any of you consider it incredible that God raises the dead?" is a valid question asked in Acts 26:8. As we have already seen, God takes no pleasure in the death of anyone (Ezekiel 18:32).

Everyone leaves this earthly life at some time, whether through death or by being taken directly into heaven (see Genesis 5:24, 2 Kings 2:11-12, Hebrews 11:5-6; 1 Thessalonians 4:16-17). God may choose to extend our earthly lives for His own purposes. We must not expect anyone, however, to live endlessly here on earth. Nor should we expect God to restore one who has died if it is not His intent or purpose to do so.

As Paul wrote to the Corinthians (1 Corinthians 15:20-24), "Christ has indeed been raised from the dead, the firstfruits of those who have fallen asleep. For since death came through a man, the resurrection of the dead comes also through a man. For as in Adam all die, so in Christ all will be made alive. But each in his own turn: Christ, the firstfruits; then, when he comes, those who belong to him."

He continues in 1 Corinthians 15:51-55: "Listen, I tell you a mystery: We will not all sleep, but we will all be changed—in a flash, in the twinkling of an eye, at the last trumpet. For the trumpet will sound, the dead will be raised imperishable, and we will be changed. For the perishable must clothe itself with the imperishable, and the mortal with immortality...."

Chapter 32

MIRACLES

———

*Definition: The special ability to effect
phenomena that cannot be explained by natural
means and that evidence a supernatural
working of God for a specific purpose*

———

Scriptures cited in Chapter 32 – Miracles

As a quality of God
Genesis 1:1-2
Revelation 4:11
Genesis 2:7
John 14:16, 25-26
1 Corinthians 15:47
Genesis 3:2-15
Exodus 10:1-2
Exodus 14:18

As illustrated in the Old Testament
Exodus 4:17
Exodus. 7:9-10
1 Kings 17:8-16
Matthew 17:9-13
Malachi 4:5
John 6:35, 48
Joshua 3:9-4:24
Joshua 6:1-20
Judges 6:16-22, 36-40
1 Kings 18:18-39
Jonah, chs 1-4

As exemplified in Jesus' ministry
John 2:1-11
Matthew 26:18
John 2:23
Matthew 8:23-27
Matthew 14:25-31
Matthew 17:24-27
Mark 6:34-44
Mark 8:2-9
Matthew 5:6
John 6:35

As illustrated in the New Testament
Acts 2:43
Acts 5:12
Acts 8:5-8
Acts 5:17-21
Mark 12:18
Acts 8:26-39
Acts 8:40
Acts 9:1-19
Acts 19:11-12

Related teachings
Exodus 10:1-2
Acts 8:9, 13, 18-24
Exodus 7:11-12
Psalm 136:2-4
Matthew 4:3-10
Ephesians 6:10-17
John 2:11
John 10:24-26

Miracles

> *Definition: The special ability to effect phenomena that cannot be explained by natural means and that evidence a supernatural working of God for a specific purpose*

As a quality of God

Even in the beginning, the Holy Spirit was involved in the miracle of creation (Genesis 1:1-2), which was accomplished by and for His will (Revelation 4:11). "The Lord formed man from the dust of the ground and he breathed into his nostrils the breath of life into him and the man became a living being" (Genesis 2:7). But notice that it wasn't until Jesus returned to heaven (John 14:16, 25-26; 1 Corinthians 15:47) that He sent His life-giving Spirit to dwell within us.

God used miracles to make Himself known—to Moses (Genesis 3:2-15), to the Israelites (Exodus 10:1-2), and to others who did not recognize Him (Exodus 14:18).

As illustrated in the Old Testament

God often chose symbolic items to exhibit miraculous signs. These included the staff of Moses (Exodus 4:17), a visible sign that could be used to indicate from a great distance the direction the group was to go, or that could be used as a focal point to call the travelers together. God even used it to exhibit His power over all creation by transforming the staff into a snake (Exodus 7:9-10).

Another example of symbolism incorporated into a miracle can be found in 1 Kings 17:8-16. Here Elijah (whom Jesus later identified in Matthew 17:9-13 as John the Baptist, the forerunner of Christ, as prophesied in Malachi 4:5) provided a widow with a continuous supply of flour and oil (often used as a symbol of the Holy Spirit) to create sustenance to nourish her, her son and Elijah with bread (symbolizing Christ, the Bread of Life, as Jesus referred to Himself in John 6:35, 48).

In Exodus 16, the immediate need was to provide nourishment for the Israelites. God again foretold His coming provision of the "Bread of Life" by providing manna. An additional purpose was to test the peoples' obedience and faith in observing His instructions.

In Joshua 3:9-4:24, the Ark of the Covenant was used to remind the Israelites of the presence of the Lord and His power to overcome seemingly insurmountable forces. Despite the River Jordan's being at flood stage, when the priests carrying the Ark stepped into the water, the waters stopped flowing until the people had crossed safely to the other side. Joshua 4:24 tells us that "He did this so that all the peoples of the earth might know that the hand of the Lord is powerful and so that you might always fear the Lord your God."

Once again the Ark was used in Joshua 6:1-20 as a symbol of God's immediate presence. They were to march (take action), blow trumpets (as to announce the coming of the King), give no war cry or raise their voices, (waiting patiently in obedience), until the signal was given to shout (rejoicing in the Lord's inevitable victory) and watching the walls of the city fall in response to their faith and obedience (observing the miracle as it occurred).

But not all miracles in the Old Testament were necessarily symbolic. When Gideon repeatedly requested confirmation that it was really God speaking to him (Judges 6:16-22, 36-40) God provided a series of miracles with the purpose of reassuring Gideon and to confirm both God's instructions and who He was.

In Elijah's showdown with the prophets of the Baals (1 Kings 18:18-39) in witness of the true God, the Lord used a miracle of countering the laws of nature to show His supreme sovereignty.

We also see God using miracles to correct and motivate disobedient servants, as we do throughout the book of Jonah (Jonah, chs. 1-3) and as object lessons to lead them to repentance (Jonah, ch. 4)

As exemplified in Jesus' ministry

Jesus first performed a miraculous sign at the wedding in Cana (John 2:1-11) by turning water into wine. Although He said it was not yet His time (v. 4; Matthew 26:18), this miracle served to manifest His glory, bringing His ministry to the attention of the public; and His disciples believed in Him (v. 14). John 2:23 tells us that during the subsequent feast of the Passover, many people observed His signs and came to believe in Him.

Although many of His miraculous works were done in public to draw people to Him, many others were done privately to inform, encourage, and strengthen the faith of His closest followers. Upon calming the winds and waves on the Sea of Galilee (Matthew 8:23-27), their astonishment opened their eyes to greater possibilities, as they wondered, "What kind of man is this? Even the winds and the waves obey Him."

Jesus took the lesson a step further, as recorded in Matthew 14:25-31, when He walked on water to intercept the disciples' storm-tossed boat. He encouraged Peter to walk to Him on the water, and caught hold of him to offer reassurance, before joining them in the boat, when Peter's faith momentarily faltered. Again He calmed the winds, for the disciples' sake further illustrating His command over natural phenomena.

The miracle described in Matthew 17:24-27 was also an assurance to the disciples of both God's character and His provision for our material and financial needs as well as for our spiritual needs.

Such provision is also evidenced in the miracles of His feeding the multitudes (Mark 6:34-44; Mark 8:2-9). By giving thanks to God for the few fish and loaves available, He was able to multiply His resources to distribute ample food to satisfy the hunger of thousands, with baskets full left over—a literal confirmation of two principles: that those who hunger and thirst for righteousness shall be filled (Matthew 5:6) and that Jesus Himself is the Bread of Life (John 6:35).

As illustrated in the New Testament

Throughout the New Testament, the many miraculous signs and wonders done by the apostles served as a witness to the people that the apostles were God's own. They gave credence to their teachings about Jesus as the Christ (Acts 2:43; Acts 5:12; Acts 8:5-8).

Even when the apostles were arrested and jailed, the Lord miraculously freed them (Acts 5:17-21) so the gospel message could reach even the Sadducees, who did not believe in life after death (Mark 12:18). Notice that the angel of the Lord told the apostles to stand in the Temple courts and give "the full message of this new life" (Acts 5:20).

God can use miracles to reach key people at the opportune time, as He did by placing Philip in the way of the Ethiopian eunuch (Acts 8:26-39) and then transporting him to Azotus to reach others (Acts 8:40). The glorified Lord also paid a miraculously visit to Saul on the road to Damascus to reveal Himself directly to the man who had been persecuting Christians (Acts 9:1-19). Following the conversion of Saul (eventually known as the Apostle Paul) God was able to do extraordinary miracles through him (Acts 19:11-12),

Related teachings

Exodus 10:1-2 tells us that God's purpose for miracles is "that you may know that I am the Lord." When what we do is based upon worldly direction, such as human will, pride, or showmanship, we are limited by the natural laws of the universe. When we act under divine direction, we know we can draw on the supernatural power of God to supersede the laws of nature, resulting in what the world terms as "a miracle."

Simon the Sorcerer was a believer (Acts 8:9, 13, 18-24). But his heart was not aligned with God's purpose. Simon wanted to aggrandize himself rather than glorifying God. He didn't understand either the character of God or the free access believers have to the Holy Spirit and His power.

Although counterfeited displays can appear to be genuine miracles, counterfeits are always weaker than genuine, God-provided miracles, as illustrated in Exodus 7:11-12. We are reminded in Psalm 136:2-4 to "Give thanks to the God of gods...to the Lord of lords ...to Him who alone does great wonders, His love endures forever."

Jesus recognized the foolishness of falling into the temptations the devil offered Him during His post-baptism fast (Matthew 4:3-10) and rejected each temptation based on the Word of God. We too must be alert to the temptations offered by the deceiver and gird ourselves with the full armor of God, including an understanding of the Word and character of God (Ephesians 6:10-17).

Miracles are Jesus' testimony of who He is (John 2:11). But even with the evidence clearly before them, some people harden their heart against Him, just as Pharaoh's heart was hardened. God responds to that by keeping them from recognizing the truth (John 10:24-26). Miracles will not make believers of all people, even though that is their purpose. We must not be discouraged if some people fail to believe in spite of them; although we can act on God's behalf to effect miracles, the result is God's work, not ours.

Chapter 33

ARTS/ CRAFTSMANSHIP

Definition: The special ability to meet a specific need through craftsmanship or an art as led by the Holy Spirit

Scriptures cited in Chapter 33 – Arts/Craftsmanship

As a quality of God
Genesis 1:1-4
Genesis 1:21, 27
Genesis 2:9
Psalm 104:30
Revelation 4:11

Related teachings
Psalm 49:1-4
Luke 10:7
Psalm 149:1-6
Proverbs 22:29

As illustrated in the Old Testament
Genesis 1:27
Exodus 31:1-5
Exodus 31:6
Proverbs 31:19, 22, 24
1 Samuel 16:15-23
2 Samuel 23:1-2
1 Chronicles 28:11-12, 19
1 Kings 4:32-33
2 Chronicles 1:11-12
Ecclesiastes 12:9-10
Ezra 1:1
Psalm 45:1

As exemplified in Jesus' ministry
Colossians 1:15-17
Ephesians 2:10
Mark 4:33
Matthew 13:10-16

As illustrated in the New Testament
Acts 9:36-39
2 Corinthians 10:1
2 Corinthians 8-11

Arts/Craftsmanship

> *Definition: The special ability to meet a specific need through craftsmanship or an art as led by the Holy Spirit*

As a quality of God

As we learn in the very first statements of Genesis (Genesis 1:1-4), God is the master artist and craftsman. It was God (the Trinity) who designed and created the heavens and the earth and all that is in them. He spoke it into being. He designed everything for function and variety, for His own pleasure, incorporating contrasts as well as similarity, consistency and balance (Genesis 1:21, 27). His designs are beautiful as well as utilitarian (Genesis 2:9).

God is not only the Creator but He shows His craftsmanship in the restoration of that creation when it deteriorates or is damaged. When He sends His Spirit, His very being, into His creation, He restores and replenishes to maintain it, reviving the earth with new soil, new life, renewed growth, and continual refreshment and revitalization (Psalm 104:30).

This extensive creativity is all for a purpose—to bring glory to Him (Revelation 4:11).

As illustrated in the Old Testament

In a similar way, since we were created in God's image (Genesis 1:27), it is reasonable to assume that He endowed us with a measure of His own creativity and craftsmanship. Yet, for specific purposes, God's Spirit provides some of His servants with an extraordinary level of creativity and skill.

When He assigned the critical work of building the Tabernacle and its furnishings, the Lord filled Bezalel with His Spirit, giving him the "skill, ability and knowledge in all kinds of crafts" that would be necessary for the demanding tasks before him (Exodus 31:1-5). This gifted artist was to refine the specific designs God had commissioned and articulate his intentions clearly to the other craftsmen. He apparently would both execute some of the work himself and oversee his assistants' work. For this reason his position demanded an extremely broad knowledge of the crafts and materials the project would require. God also gifted Oholiab with the skills necessary to assist Bezalel, though we may assume that his gifting did not cover exactly the same ground—possibly it was less creative but placed a stronger emphasis on a supporting gift such as helps or administration. We cannot know specifically what gifts he was given; but we do know that God Spiritually gifted him to fulfill his responsibilities in assisting Bezalel. Though the craftsmen who worked under these men to construct the commissioned furnishings were gifted with the skills of craftsmanship, they were not, apparently, gifted as extensively, or at least in the same areas as those who would direct the work (Exodus 31:6).

These craftsmen were given skills to use a variety of materials. Unlike Bezalel, who was gifted in skill with all of the work he would be overseeing, their skills were probably limited to one or two specific areas of expertise, such as woodworking, metallurgy and smithing, tool making, cabinetry, masonry, textiles, needlework, or jewelry making. These skills might be considered commensurate with today's commercial design, engineering, and manufacture in a wide variety of fields. Yet, whatever the gifts, however extensive any one person's may have been, all the artists and craftsmen worked together to accomplish the work the Lord had set before them.

Needlework and its related industries in the field of textiles, such as spinning and weaving, are additional forms of craftsmanship specifically mentioned (Proverbs 31:19, 22, 24) as meeting needs on a commercial level as well as on a smaller, private scale.

Another art that is widely used in God's service is music. David is perhaps the most readily recognized of the musicians in the Old Testament. When King Saul's spirit was troubled, young David was commissioned to play his harp to soothe him. Through God's gifting, this music therapy calmed the king and opened the door for David to be invited into the king's continuing service (1 Samuel 16:15-23). David later described himself as "Israel's singer of songs," saying "The Spirit of the Lord spoke through me, His word was on my tongue" (2 Samuel 23:1-2). He was musically gifted not only in instrumental music but also in singing and psalm writing.

Yet David's artistic gifts were not limited to music. He was apparently also gifted in architectural design and draftsmanship (1 Chronicles 28:11-12, 19), which he readily acknowledged as from the Lord.

David's son Solomon was artistically gifted, as well, notably as a journalist and poet. Solomon used his gifts to express his appreciation, understanding, and knowledge of God's creation through his writings (1 Kings 4:32-33). The Holy Spirit provided the wisdom and understanding (2 Chronicles 1:11-12) that enabled Solomon to research and write about the flora and fauna of his land. Solomon also used his journalistic gift to write, compile, and edit books of proverbs and songs. He wrote the equivalent of today's textbooks. He was endued by the Holy Spirit with knowledge, wisdom in how to present the information at his disposal, and precision and accuracy in his compilations (Ecclesiastes 12:9-10), with evidence of careful craftsmanship.

It is interesting to note that not only believers in God can be empowered by the Holy Spirit to accomplish God's purposes. Cyrus, king of Persia, was empowered by God in order to fulfill the prophecy of Jeremiah (Ezra 1:1). He used his God-given position as king to proclaim God's word through public speaking and a written proclamation.

Public speaking, in the form of oral narration, is mentioned again in Psalm 45:1, in which the psalmist recognizes his tongue as "the pen of a skillful writer." Perhaps he regularly served as an oral historian or compiled current news for the king's edification and entertainment; in any case, his gift was used to compose and sing poetry that brought glory to God.

As exemplified in Jesus' ministry

Jesus is the visible form of the invisible heavenly Father. He was the first of the Father's creation; all else was created by Him (Colossians 1:15-17).

The triune God designed and created us. Christ did the finishing work, preparing us for useful service (Ephesians 2:10) according to the plan and will of God.

Jesus' artistic gift is apparent particularly in the art of storytelling. Every parable He told had a central lesson to convey. Yet all were told in such a way that their depth was perceived only to the degree of the listeners' ability and willingness to understand. Those listeners with closed hearts and minds could not understand beyond the most superficial facts of the stories; those with hearts enlightened by Spiritual understanding were able to benefit from the more profound lessons embedded in the parables (Mark 4:33; Matthew 13:10-16).

As illustrated in the New Testament

The art and craft of needlework provided an important contribution to the Church in Joppa. The congregation was so impressed with Tabitha's handiwork that it is reasonable to suppose that her gifted craftsmanship in needlework may have been one of the ways she "was always doing good and helping the poor" (Acts 9:36-39).

Paul, too, applied his artistic gift to reach the extended Church and across the generations to us even today. Although Paul was apparently not a notably forceful speaker, he was unquestionably a skilled and gifted writer whose letters still speak with the voice of God's authority (2 Corinthians 10:1, 8-11). The gift of specific arts and craftsmanship may not have been specifically named in the New Testament text, but it is extensively illustrated in the actual writing and compilation of the biblical text.

Related teachings

When the Lord reveals something to an artisan, the artist, in turn, uses his understanding of it to express it to others, through his or her art, in such a way that will open others' hearts to the message (Psalm 49:1-4). We should pay attention to those messages God reveals to us through the arts. Such arts are not limited to music, dance, writing, and visual arts, but may include other performance arts, practical arts such as architecture, and various forms of industrial design and craftsmanship, as well. Any skill that requires creativity and careful workmanship may be gifted by the Holy Spirit in this way.

When God provides us with the services of a Spiritually gifted artisan, He expects the Church to appreciate and apply their craft in such a way as to bring Him glory. And the artist, like any laborer, should expect to be compensated for his or her contributions (Luke 10:7). God delights in creativity on His behalf and provides songs and dances through skilled artists for the benefit of all the Church, so that we may all give Him pleasure through our united praises (Psalm 149:1-6). Congregations should feel free to incorporate new songs into their praise services to God and to rejoice and follow the lead of gifted musicians and choreographers in praising our Lord.

Those skilled in the arts and in various forms of craftsmanship through Spiritual gifting will be recognized and placed in positions that will permit them to use those gifts in service to the King of all kings. Their service may appear to be before obscure men, but only God can know whom their influence will touch or how far it will reach. God gifts His people in order that, through service to others, they may serve Him, greatest of all the kings anyone could be called upon to serve (Proverbs 22:29).

Chapter 34

MISSIONS

Definition: The special ability to successfully use one's other Spiritual gifts to minister to people in a cultural situation different from one's own

---

Scriptures cited in Chapter 34 – Missions

As a quality of God
1Timothy 2:4-8
2 Chronicles 6:32-35
Acts 10:34-35
Isaiah 61:11
Acts 15:7-9

Related teachings
Psalm 105:1-4
Acts 26:22-23
Luke 18:29-30
Matthew 6:33
Psalm 25:25
Psalm 118:26
Psalm 126:6
Acts 9:15
Ephesians 3:7-9

As illustrated in the Old Testament
Jonah, chs 1-4
Isaiah 65:1-5
Isaiah 66:18-21
Zechariah 2:10-11
Zechariah 9:10
Romans 11:2-32

As exemplified in Jesus' ministry
Luke 19:2-10
Luke 3:8
Romans 4:8-17
Matthew 15:21-28
Mark 7:24-29
Matthew 28:18-19

As illustrated in the New Testament
Acts 8:4-8
Acts 8:26-38
Acts 16:6-10
Acts 26:15-18
Galatians 2:2
Galatians 2:7-10
Acts 11:15-18
Acts 11:19-21
Acts 14:26-28
Acts 21:17-20
Acts 13:45-49
Acts 18:6-8

Chapter 34

Missions

> *Definition: The special ability to successfully use one's other Spiritual gifts to minister to people in a cultural situation different from one's own*

As a quality of God

God's purpose for missions (and in all His dealings with all nations, through both confrontations and reprieves) is that all people will recognize and honor Him as the One God, the Sovereign Lord and will recognize Christ as the Savior, the embodiment of God's grace, the ultimate reprieve (1 Timothy 2:4-8).

When Solomon prayed in 2 Chronicles 6:32-35, he knew it was already a characteristic of God to reach out with mercy and grace to foreigners as well as to His own people; he called on God to hear their prayers to Him so that all people of the earth would know His name and fear Him (v. 33). Although as he prayed regarding "when your people go to war" he was probably thinking militarily, the concept also refers to spiritual warfare against the devil (v. 34), in any locale. Again he pleaded that God would hear from heaven and uphold their (righteous) cause, with forgiveness for those who acknowledge their sins and repent (v. 39).

Peter recognized in Acts 10:34-35 that God chooses whom He will save, that we do not have the right to deny anyone the opportunity of salvation. For, "as the soil makes the sprout come up and a garden causes seeds to grow, so the Sovereign LORD will make righteousness and praise spring up before all nations" (Isaiah 61:11). International missions are effective because of the Lord's will and intent that all people should come to know Him. In Acts 15:7-9, Peter again reported that God showed His acceptance of the Gentiles by giving them the Holy Spirit, making no distinction between Jews and Gentiles whose hearts He had purified by faith.

As illustrated in the Old Testament

If nations or individuals follow their own will, they face conflict, loss, and despair; if they follow God in whole-hearted obedience, they find reprieve, satisfaction, peace, and hope. We see this throughout the Old Testament—Genesis, Exodus, Daniel,… However, Jonah's obedience was not whole-hearted (Jonah, chs 1-4), so he did not enjoy the satisfaction he could have found in having succeeded in God's mission; he begrudged Ninevah's salvation, so he himself lost hope. Jonah could not forgive Ninevah's past offences toward his people, so he found no peace even in the reprieve God had granted to him after his initial defiance.

Isaiah 65:1-5 tells us that although God initially revealed Himself to the Jews, in general they did not accept Him, preferring to go their own way, in opposition to His authority. So, as we see in Isaiah 66:18-21, God reached out to other nations that were more willing to recognize and honor Him. From those people He would designate some for ministry and would delegate other believers to proclaim His glory even further abroad.

As the Lord declared in Zechariah 2:10-11, "Many nations will be joined with the LORD in that day and will become my people. I will live among you and you will know that the LORD Almighty has sent me to you." Zechariah 9:10 continues, "His rule will extend from sea to sea and from the River to the ends of the earth."

It is interesting to note that the term "Daughter of Zion," as used in Zechariah 2:10-11 and Zechariah 9:9-10, refers to the spiritual offspring of those claiming the sanctuary of God's protection (Zion). This, as we will see in Romans 11:2-32, will include "wild olive shoots" (of any Gentile culture) grafted into the "cultivated olive root" of Christ.

As exemplified in Jesus' ministry

Jesus singled out Zacchaeus, a sinful, Gentile tax collector, from the crowd attempting to see Him (Luke 19:2-10) to invite Himself into his home. When Zacchaeus took the opportunity to receive Jesus and repent of his sins, Jesus acknowledged him as a new "son of Abraham. For the Son of Man came to seek and save what was lost." As Jesus had told the crowd in Luke 3:8, "descendants" from Abraham are determined not by bloodlines or nationality but by one's true relationship to God, through repentance and the righteousness of faith (Romans 4:8-17).

As recorded in both Matthew 15:21-28 and Mark 7:24-29, although Jesus had been sent specifically to the Jews, many of whom continued to reject Him, He acknowledged and honored the faith of the Gentile woman when she sought His healing for her daughter.

The great commission that Jesus gave to His followers (Matthew 28:18-19) was to go to all nations—nations being not just geographical areas but cultures—to make Him known to the lost.

As illustrated in the New Testament

Both Ethiopian and Samarian society were culturally very different from what Philip knew, yet he was effective in ministering to both peoples. Acts 8:4-8 tells us that his mission work in Samaria was accompanied by miracles, driving out of spirits, and healings because they were able to give credence to what he was saying as he proclaimed Christ there. Philip later evangelized and baptized an Ethiopian eunuch whom he encountered in the desert (Acts 8:26-38).

Like Paul, some of whose travels we find recorded in Acts 16:6-10, missionaries must be sensitive to God's direction and must be obedient in following His guidance to be most effective in their missions. They are commissioned by God to go where He sends them and to whom He sends them, as we see in Acts 26:15-18.

Although called and commissioned by God, missionaries must also maintain accountability to the Church body to verify that they are accurately sensing the Holy Spirit's leading, as the Apostle Paul did (Galatians 2:2).

We are reminded in Galatians 2:7-10 that each missionary is called to a field of God's choosing—different for each, but with the same purpose—to make known to the lost the saving gospel of Jesus Christ and to be representatives of the grace of God on earth.

In Acts 11:15-18, the Apostle Peter reminded his fellow Jewish believers that, if God is gracious enough to save and baptize Gentiles with the Holy Spirit, it is not the right of anyone else who has received that saving grace to oppose Him.

We read in Acts 11:19-21 that some believers who had scattered in fear when Stephen was martyred carried the gospel message only to Jews. But believers from other areas were extending the message to the Greeks, as well. "The Lord's hand was with them," Acts 11:21 tells us, "and a great number of people believed and turned to the Lord."

Acts 14:26-28 and Acts 21:17-20 indicate that reports of progress and success are encouraging and refreshing for both the home church and those emissaries who are sent, as they recognize how God has moved through their joint efforts.

Not everyone appreciated the apostles' message. As we read in Acts 13:45-49, the Jews became jealous and abusive. "Paul and Barnabas answered them boldly: "We had to speak the word of God to you first. Since you reject it and do not consider yourselves worthy of eternal life, we now turn to the Gentiles. For this is what the Lord has commanded us: 'I have made you a light for the Gentiles, that you may bring salvation to the ends of the earth.'"

They opposed Paul similarly in Acts 18:6-8. He shook out his clothes in protest, and said to them, "Your blood be on your own heads! I am clear of my responsibility. From now on I will go to the Gentiles."

Related teachings

Psalm 105:1-4 reminds us to "Give thanks to the LORD, call on his name; make known among the nations what he has done. Sing to him, sing praise to him; tell of all his wonderful acts. Glory in his holy name; let the hearts of those who seek the LORD rejoice. Look to the LORD and his strength; seek his face always."

The message Paul taught, as he wrote in Acts 26:22-23, is "saying nothing beyond what the prophets and Moses said would happen—that the Christ would suffer and, as the first to rise from the dead, would proclaim light to his own people and to the Gentiles."

God provides recompense for those who sacrifice personal comfort and relationships for the sake of the kingdom of God (Luke 18:29-30; Matthew 6:33).

The gospel provides welcome hope for the lost in all lands (Psalm 25:25) and a blessing to those who carry it to others (Psalm 118:26; Psalm 126:6).

The obedience Ananias displayed in response to the Lord's commission to seek out Saul in Acts 9:15 has proven to be world-changing. Even if our own gifts do not include missions, and we don't understand God's methods, we are still to be obedient in using our gifts to help Him carry them out through others. Because of Ananias's obedience, Saul/Paul "became a servant of this gospel by the gift of God's grace given ... to preach to the Gentiles the unsearchable riches of Christ, and to make plain to everyone the administration of this mystery..." (Ephesians 3:7-9).

Afterword

Learning from the Master Teacher,
the Author and Perfecter of our faith

I was almost thirty when I gave my heart to Christ and was born again. Having been raised largely in interdenominational chapels because my military family moved frequently, and influenced also by my mother's missionary heritage and my father's encouragement to join church choirs, I certainly knew *about* Jesus and continually asked Him to lead me, but in all those years I hadn't met Him personally.

Soon after our marriage, my husband and I began attending a new church, where the gifts of the Spirit were very evident and actively used. I had never been so aware of them and had been led to believe that most of them were no longer active.

Suddenly I was eager to know more about them—both what gifts I might have and how to use them. The only books I could find that purported to discuss the Spiritual gifts seemed insufficient to me, and even those that offered to help identify our gifts seemed very limited— and limiting in their range and expectations. I wanted to attend a class where we could explore the topic in greater depth and share our experiences with gifts used in the present day. But no such classes were being offered at that time in our church.

"Teach the class, yourself," I heard the Lord telling me day after day.

"But what do I know about Spiritual gifts?" I prayed. I was at it again, arguing with the Lord. It wasn't the first time. Several years earlier He had called me into the ministry, but I had argued with Him about that, as well. (As a mother of three young children, whose husband was rarely home, I didn't feel I could commit to study at a seminary, and the home study course I began fell by the wayside in lieu of all the interruptions and distractions I faced.)

Although God always knows what He's talking about; neither of these calls seemed reasonable—or believable—to me at the time. So I argued. And now He was telling me to teach a class on a subject about which I knew little.

Further argument was pointless. He'd win anyway; He usually does. I knew I might as well agree to teach the class. …But I would rather be a student in that class. That seemed much easier, to be handed all the information I wanted, and it would take so much less of my time!

But … "What textbook should I use?" I asked God in resignation.

"Everything you need to know is in the Bible," The Lord told me.

Of course it was in the Bible! But what? No other textbook? I could think of only two, three, maybe four books in the New Testament that had much to say about Spiritual gifts. But if He said "It's all in the Bible," I knew it must be. But how could I possibly find enough to teach for a full Sunday School quarter?

Then the Lord reminded me not to take this responsibility lightly.

So, well, okay: I had the commission; I had the textbook. But I didn't have the time, I reminded Him. My husband and I were in the process of buying a new house, several states away, and that would eat heavily into any spare time I might have in the coming months. I'd be gone for several weekends in each of the upcoming Sunday School quarters; it wouldn't be fair to make the commitment to teach when I knew I'd be gone a large portion of the time. (I found lots of excuses.)

"Use this quarter to prepare," the Lord told me. With ambivalent feelings I acknowledged that I'd better do so. I knew from experience that He would work out the schedule, and I would need to be ready when it all fell into place.

The next hurdle was to approach our pastor about teaching an adult Sunday School class. "Why do you feel the Lord wants you to teach it?" he asked. Would even our pastor believe that God actually speaks to me? Even after I admitted that I had no idea yet how to even approach the subject, he said, somewhat to my surprise, "We'll schedule you for the fall quarter. You'll need to talk with the adult Sunday School superintendent about finding a classroom. And I'll want to see any materials you plan to hand out to the class."

As simple as that? Well, not quite. I'd discovered once again how readily the Lord can open doors, but I still had to do my own homework. My teaching would be inextricably linked to my studies. I still needed to learn everything I intended to teach the class.

But where should I start? I had scarcely a clue. I knew that I Corinthians talked about Spiritual gifts, and Acts would shed some additional light on the subject, but I had no idea of the questions I would need to find answers to. I didn't really know what to look for; nor did I have any concrete ideas about how the course should be organized.

I started to list questions I wanted answered for myself: How had Jesus used the power that was available to Him during His earthly ministry? How had the early Church applied Spiritual gifts to their work? And how would all that translate into our using them within the Church today?

A pocket-sized Bible accompanied me as I flew back and forth between home and the new house, so I could use the flights and waiting time to begin my reading. I began with the Gospel of Matthew and was astonished at the number of traits, which we would consider in ourselves to be Spiritual gifts, that Jesus used in His ministry. I began to list them—not only miracles and healings, but leadership, teaching, administration, encouragement, words of knowledge and wisdom, exhortation, mercy, pastoring, poverty, intercession, faith—as I scoured the New Testament. I highlighted and made note of applicable scripture passages. Soon the Old Testament revealed even more teachings about these gifts of the Holy Spirit—more than I could ever have imagined.

With new realizations came new insights, new questions to answer, and new hypotheses to trace as I continued to read. A course outline began slowly to take shape.

I found myself listening as Jesus taught His disciples about using the gifts we would be given and about the attitude of love with which they should be used. I sat at His feet as He taught us how to teach, how to pray; I watched from his side as He showed us how to heal, how to serve, how to encourage... I received His instructions, along with the others, when He sent them out on their own to preach and heal and learn from experience. And I began to realize that I was learning as much from His example, and from their experience, as from His words.

He was teaching me further about Spiritual gifts by making me stretch my faith in His guidance, by showing me His power in seemingly risky circumstances, and by making me more acutely aware of the gifts that His Holy Spirit was stirring up within *me*. Besides all that, He was teaching me how to study and was allowing me to rediscover the joy of making continual new discoveries in His Word.

He is the Author and the Perfecter of our faith (Hebrews 12:2). From what other author's book could I more effectively teach? From whom could I learn any better? He had begun an ongoing process of transforming me into the student I never was in school. Our Lord is indeed the Master Teacher.

After teaching the class, I still felt called to continue the Spiritual gifts study to make it available for the general public. I expanded the scope of the study for each gift, breaking each down into five segments.

But in the midst of raising a family, my husband's retirement, several home relocations, and other distractions, this study, too, eventually became sidelined, incomplete. I felt God's repeated call to return to it, but it became one of those tasks I would get back to "someday."

More than twenty years later, the neglected manuscript still languished unfinished. And I began to feel some infirmities that I chalked up to advancing age. But after all, I supposed that I would have many more years to return to the study. So I didn't heed the repeated nudge to resume the work ... until I received a preliminary diagnosis from my doctor that I was in the early stages of a degenerative disease that could eventually totally incapacitate me before it claimed my life. No one could estimate how much time I might have left. I felt a bit like Jonah, having gotten a drastic wake-up call to obey God and complete what He had called me to accomplish.

Suddenly God's long-standing call became my first priority.

Doctors offered no hope for healing or even assurance of being able to slow progression of the disease. My only hope was in God.

What did the Bible say about healing? Suddenly the Word became immediate to my situation. I dove into the Bible to bolster my faith, find encouragement, and understand God's purposes for both permitting disease and providing healing. I needed a greater understanding of the gifts as they manifested themselves within me and as others were used to my benefit—mercy, helps, intercession, faith, hospitality, and so many more. Was God's will to heal me or did He have a higher purpose, beyond drawing me closer to Him and back to the task at hand? I began to see spiritual reawakening in the people around me as we faced new challenges together.

The Bible held many of the answers I needed. I knew I was in the midst of spiritual warfare. Would this cup pass from me as I asked, or would it serve a greater purpose if I, like the Apostle Paul, were to allow God's power and grace to be magnified through my weakness? It isn't up to me; it's up to God. Whether as a living testimony of God's faithfulness or whether unto death, could this be the gift of martyrdom that had been spoken of me many years ago, which I had discounted as unlikely and had forgotten? It has certainly helped me understand the gift of lifetime martyrdom as I confidently leave my health entirely in God's hands, willing to be used for His purposes, whatever it may mean for my own life. Healing will happen, whether in this temporal life or in the eternal life to come.

As I resumed the work, He provided me with deeper understanding of many of the gifts, guiding me, building my faith through His Word, and encouraging me, which reinforced my faith even further.

Meanwhile, a host of friends were holding me up in prayer. Not doubting that the Lord *could* heal me but uncertain of His ultimate purposes in this situation, I asked God that I at least be given time to complete the work He had called me to do. As I write now, I trust that, with the guidance and grace of the Holy Spirit, and the forgiveness and redemption through Christ Jesus, the work will be completed and will find its way to publication, not because of my obedience, but despite my *dis*obedience, simply because it's the will of God, who wants it made available to His Church.

I pray that this study will prove a blessing to many and will continue to strengthen the Church as more Christians discover and apply their Spiritual gifts to glorify God and Christ our Savior, who has given us the benefit of His own Holy Spirit, to live and work both within and through us to His glory.

Charlotte E. Mertz
July 2023

Printed in the United States
by Baker & Taylor Publisher Services